SQUARE PEGS, ROUND HOLES

SQUARE PEGS, ROUND HOLES

The Learning-Disabled Child
in the Classroom and at Home

by HAROLD B. LEVY, M.D.

LITTLE, BROWN AND COMPANY — BOSTON — TORONTO

E

Simulated WISC items included in this book are used by
permission of The Psychological Corporation. Material based
on the ITPA test is used by permission of Dr. Samuel A.
Kirk.

Library of Congress Cataloging in Publication Data

Levy, Harold B
  Square pegs, round holes.

  Bibliography: p.
  1. Mentally handicapped children--Education.
2. Problem children--Education. I. Title.
LC4661.L42   371.9'2   73-3422
ISBN 0-316-52232-5
ISBN 0-316-52233-3 (pbk.)

*Published simultaneously in Canada
by Little, Brown & Company (Canada) Limited*

PRINTED IN THE UNITED STATES OF AMERICA

To the eight million square pegs throughout this country, for their courage and determination — and to their parents and teachers for theirs.

CONTENTS

FOREWORD

Dr. Levy's book is a gratifying, much-needed contribution to the burgeoning literature on specific learning disabilities. It is rewarding to find a physician taking time out from his pediatric practice to write with such insight, not about a pathological condition but about the children who have it. It is obvious that Dr. Levy has taken the time to learn from his patients and their parents. His book shows keen insight into the behavioral as well as the physiological aspects of "minimal brain dysfunction," yet he has resisted the trend to write scientifically for professionals or emotionally for parents. From a pediatrician's years of experience in diagnosing and treating children with specific learning disabilities, Harold B. Levy, M.D. speaks for such children to their physicians, parents and teachers.

The medical profession has long been aware of specific learning disabilities, especially as they affect a child's acquisition of the language faculty. Educators, however, have been slow to manifest such awareness. Teachers continue to assume uniformity of behavior and academic learning among children. Dr. Levy explains in well-chosen terms that academic learning is dependent upon integrity of the central nervous system, and that children with minimal brain dysfunction will exhibit behavioral deviations. His book represents an appeal from medicine to pedagogy to recognize and accept a group of children heretofore misunderstood and consequently mismanaged. He points out the prevalence of specific learning disabilities, but he discourages those who would be case-finding agents for the purpose of referring problem-children out of the educational mainstream.

Parents will find comfort and relief from feelings of guilt about their children with specific learning disorders when they read this book. New insights into cause and effective treatment are given.

Though Dr. Levy's book is addressed to parents and teachers, he is ever mindful of the interests of children. His book might be expected to stem the growing epidemic of specific learning disabilities which afflicts so many otherwise "normal" children.

Empress Y. Zedler, Ph.D.
Chairman, Department of
          Special Education
Southwest Texas State University
San Marcos, Texas

ACKNOWLEDGMENTS

No book such as this is ever the work of just one man, and this one is certainly no exception. The impressions and concepts that appear on the pages to follow represent the results of conversations and discussions with many individuals with whom I have shared for many years a mutual interest in the problems of learning-disabled children.

My first encounters with these difficulties came through work at the Caddo School for Exceptional Children where I was introduced to perceptual disorders and remedial techniques by two remarkable young women, Joan Harrington, a speech pathologist, and Nancy Rachel, an occupational therapist. These talented and devoted members of the staff developed their own methods of identification and correction at a time when very little was understood about the scope and frequency of learning disabilities. We were joined in our studies at the Caddo School in those early days by William G. Fellman, whose optometric training had grounded him in a thorough understanding of visual-motor disturbances which allowed him to make a valuable contribution to our children before his altogether too untimely passing.

Under the auspices of the Caddo Foundation, I attended the postgraduate course in neuromuscular disorders conducted by the pioneer pediatric neurologist, Meyer Perlstein, and through the sponsorship of this outstanding teacher and great humanitarian I was accepted for membership in the American Academy for Cerebral Palsy. Attendance at the meetings of this remarkable multi-disciplinary organization gave me the privilege of discussing developmental and learning disorders with such early authorities as Arnold Gesell, Alfred Strauss, Edgar Doll, and Richmond Paine, all of them, like Dr. Perlstein, now gone, but of unforgettable memory for their legacy to handicapped children. At present I have the opportunity of working with such current leaders in the field as Eric Denhoff, William Cruickshank, and Elena Boder, with whom the reader will soon become acquainted.

Here at home my understanding of the problems of the learning-disabled child has been aided considerably by association with Otha King Miles and Dorothy Bird Gwin of Centenary College, with Ralph Frybarger in speech pathology, and with Pat Harrington, husband of the aforementioned Joan and a contributor to the field in his own right. Hyman Gardsbane has taken up the torch left by Bill Fellman and extended our horizons through his work with the Association for Children with Learning Disabilities, of which he is past national president. For much of the material on present educational and emotional concepts I am indebted to Michael Counihan of Del Mar College, to Sol Gordon of Syracuse University, and especially to Empress Young Zedler of Southwest Texas State University, who evaluated this manuscript and kindly consented to write the foreword.

The actual mechanisms of bringing this book into

being required the skillful co-operation of a number of other capable individuals. At Little, Brown I first met Lin Richter and Ralph Woodward, who counselled with me and guided me in the right direction. John Keller, my editor, has been of inestimable assistance with his patience and understanding, as has been Lee Workum. Their professional expertise would be obvious to anyone who had followed this work from its awkward beginnings to the finished product. I am especially grateful that they had enough confidence in me not to assign an "as-told-to" writer, but allowed me to have my say, even though that decision must have made their tasks immeasurably more difficult.

My local medical colleagues have been a welcome source of assistance and encouragement. A. L. Wedgeworth, Jr., and Frank Jobe in pediatrics, Peter Boggs and Bettina Hillman Mattson in allergy, Donald Texada in ophthalmology, Andrew Mullen and Charles Armistead in neuropsychiatry, Doug King in obstetrics, and Albert Hand in pathology all have willingly shared their ideas, their experiences, and their professional libraries with me, for which I am most appreciative.

But this book would have never been possible were it not for the remarkable devotion and capabilities of Kathryn Delouche, who handled the almost unbelievable task of translating my handwriting into intelligible English while at the same time managing a pediatric office and the many duties this involved. The actual completed manuscript was the work of Martha Dudley, aided by Cathey Roos Cook. The bibliography reflects the concerned interest of Rae Colvard, librarian at the Confederate Memorial Medical Center, and the staff of the LSU School of Medicine Library in Shreveport. To all these fine people I am grateful almost beyond expression.

Most of all this book has been a family endeavor. From the time my son Jim opened the door at Little, Brown, he and Carolyn, Chuck and Anita, and Roger and Judy have contributed so much by their enthusiasm and advice. And behind them has been their wonderful mother, who so skillfully blended her roles as benevolent taskmaster and patient helpmate. Without her patience during my moments of impatience and her inspiration during my hours of discouragement this book could never have been completed. It is as much her work as mine.

And, finally, the parents of all the learning-disabled children with whom I have been privileged to work deserve special mention here. They, together with the teachers and counselors, as well as their children themselves, have taught me most of what appears in the ensuing pages. The credit for whatever of value the reader may derive from this book must be shared with them as well as all the wonderful people mentioned previously. The responsibility for the deficiencies found belongs to the author alone.

HAROLD B. LEVY, M.D.

SQUARE PEGS, ROUND HOLES

PROLOGUE:
THE SAGA OF STEVE

When Steve came to my office for the first time, he appeared to be a personable eleven-year-old youngster who cooperated well throughout his examination, answering all my questions politely, obviously trying to please. He seemed a bit amused at my request to draw pictures and write the note that completed his examination, but readily turned to his tasks while his mother and I crossed the hall to the consultation room. There, after a few preliminary questions about Steve's birth history and developmental progress, we began to talk about his educational experiences. Our dialogue went something like this:

"When did you first suspect Steve was having trouble?"

"Actually, he's had trouble ever since the first grade. We couldn't afford to send him to a private kindergarten, and the town in which we were living didn't have any kindergartens in the public school system. We probably shouldn't have started Steve when we did, but his birthday was in late September, and, since he was rather large for his age, we entered him in the first grade just before he was six. Several of his little friends from our neighborhood were starting at the same time, and he had been looking forward eagerly to going along with them. Steve had always been so inquisitive and seemed to be such a bright child to his father and me, asking questions about everything and appearing to us so anxious to learn, that we couldn't believe his teacher when she told us later on that year that he wasn't doing well in school. She said he wouldn't listen to her in the classroom and didn't seem interested in what was taking place, that he couldn't sit still in his seat, pay attention, or remember her instructions. But she reassured us that she had dealt with many boys just like him and told us to *leave him alone*, since he would probably outgrow it, so she passed him on to the second grade."

"And what happened then?"

"Well, it was more of the same the next year. His second-grade teacher noticed he was having a lot of trouble with his reading, and suggested we have *his eyes checked*, but the doctor told us he had perfect vision. He said that maybe Steve had *a hearing problem*, so we went to the ear doctor who reported no problem there either. We noticed that Steve would often read things backwards, like 'was' for 'saw' and 'tap' for 'pat,' and would even write some of his letters or numbers in reverse. When we asked his teacher about it, she told us that many children did this when they first started reading and writing — that it was just another sign of Steve's *immaturity*. In nearly every conference we had, she kept referring to his being so immature and suggested that I was an overprotective mother. She even told me that if I would just cut the apron strings and let Steve grow up he would do so much better, since she had known of other children just like him who were *late bloomers*. We finished the year on a friendly basis — she told me she knew Steve had a lot more potential than he showed and passed him to the third grade."

"And then?"

"And then the roof fell in. Doctor, you wouldn't believe what happened to us. Stevie's third-grade teacher had been in the same school for thirty years and prided herself on being a strict disciplinarian. She insisted that her pupils have a solid foundation, and when Steve wouldn't finish his assignments, she urged us to put more pressure on him at home, since he just seemed to be *lazy*. She told us to take away some of his privileges until he developed proper study habits. The stricter she became in the classroom, the more Steve would act up, and the worse his grades became. His teacher thought that his previous teachers might have overestimated his ability, and suggested we have Steve evaluated to see if he might be a *slow learner* or even a bit *retarded*."

"What did the evaluation show?"

"Actually, they wouldn't tell my husband and me much of anything. It was all very hush-hush, but I did happen to steal a look at one report on the teacher's desk that gave Steve an IQ rating of 124. His teacher didn't seem to believe this, but told me that Steve might have some sort of *emotional block* that was preventing him from learning. She said Steve was obviously a very nervous child, and at her insistence we took him to the Child Guidance Center."

"And how did things go there?"

"That was the worst six months of our lives. They told us that, while Steve did indeed have normal intelligence, his overactivity in the classroom was being caused by something we were doing wrong as his parents. They asked us all sorts of questions about our family life, and, while we tried to co-operate with them, how would you feel if someone told you, 'All your child needs is someone at home who really loves him'? My husband refused to go back after the social worker asked him about how much he drank and did he go around with other women, but I hoped they would help my child, so I kept on going. They would have Steve kick over wooden blocks and break balloons to get rid of his 'suppressed hostility,' but after six months he still couldn't read and we could hardly control him after he came home from one of these sessions. Finally, one day I went to pick him up and found they were having Steve and all the other children drop balloons filled with water from the second-story windows on the passers-by below — and that was the last straw! I agreed with my husband, and we stopped going there. We talked to our family doctor who told us to quit worrying so much, that we both were overly concerned, and that he would prescribe a *tranquilizer* for the boy, but that we were the ones who really needed it. The medicine just made Steve sleepy all day, so we had to stop it."

"How were things going at school?"

"Steve's teacher was quite upset when we didn't follow through with the Guidance Center, and told us it would be wrong to pass him, since he obviously wasn't ready for the fourth grade. We all agreed it would be better for him to *repeat the year*, and since we had learned that my husband's company was transferring him to another town, we felt this would be the right time to do it."

"And how did that work out?"

"Things started out much better that next year. Steve's new teacher was a young lady just a year or so out of college and seemed to know something about how to cope with his problem. She put his seat right next to her desk, and even worked with him after school. His reading seemed to improve, but his handwriting and spelling remained terrible. His teacher noticed that Steve seemed to do better with oral recitations than with written tests, so she suggested that we let him read aloud more to us at home. She told us he still fidgeted a lot in the classroom, but she seemed to tolerate him."

"So things were improving?"

"Very much so — but, just our luck, his teacher had to drop out at mid-term for maternity leave. His new teacher soon informed us that with thirty-two other children in the classroom she just didn't have time to give any one child special attention, especially one who was obviously an *underachiever*. When Steve began to act up and disrupt the class, she started sending him down to the principal's office quite frequently. Steve began to have fights in school, and the principal asked my husband's permission to use *physical punishment*. When he refused, they had some heated words, and we all had a touchy month until school was out. But at least they passed him on to the fourth grade."

"And then?"

"We sent Steve to *summer school* because we knew he

was reading so poorly, but I really don't know how much good it did. I think Steve felt we were punishing him since we didn't let him go to Boy Scout camp because his school work was so bad. When school took up again in the fall we had high hopes that things would finally get better, but Steve's reputation must have been passed along, for his new teacher told us she had heard all about him and that she wasn't going to put up with a *troublemaker*. She started sending notes home with Steve about his misbehaving, and half the time we would never get them because Steve would forget them or lose them on the way home. When we didn't reply to them his teacher said we were typical modern parents who weren't really interested in our children. I tried to explain all we had done, and that by that time I had two other small children at home, but I don't think she really believed me. She did suggest that we get a *tutor* to help Steve, but we had a hard time finding one who was qualified. Steve seemed to enjoy spending the time with his tutor, even though it cut into his after-school play time. We managed to make it through the school year, and once again my husband's company saw fit to transfer him in his job, this time to Shreveport."

"And how are things going this year?"

"Not good at all. Steve has been in the fifth grade just one month and he's already in trouble. He knows he is older and larger than most of the children in his room, and he seems very sensitive to their remarks about him. He says he has no friends, that the other boys pick on him, and that he always is the one who gets blamed for anything that happens in his room, whether it is his fault or not. He got into a fight on the playground yesterday with one of the boys who Steve says called him stupid and retarded, so the principal *suspended him* from school and told him not to come back until he had learned to control himself and get along with others. Doctor, what are we going to do?"

With that question there was a knock on the door and Steve came in with his drawings and his note. The drawings were rather well done, but the distorted handwriting and garbled spelling were obviously inconsistent with the manner in which Steve had spoken to me and expressed himself orally. I sent him back to work the puzzles which are part of our evaluation, and began to discuss with his mother what I felt was the cause of her son's problem. I explained how we now recognize that children like him have a chemical disturbance which affects the way in which their nervous systems process the information they receive, that we call this condition *minimal brain dysfunction*, and that the difficulties in school are known as *specific learning disabilities*. She listened attentively as we covered the importance of the secondary emotional effects on the child's personality that resulted from the frustration and humiliation to which he was subjected in the classroom. When the question of medication arose, she was able to understand the reasons for its use and readily agreed to try anything that might help her boy.

We ended on such an affable note that I wasn't prepared for the resentment that came out in her final question: "But, Doctor, why didn't someone tell me all of this before now? Why did we have to subject Steve to those five years of what must have been a living hell for him? Not one of his teachers, not one of the psychologists, the principal, our family doctor — *no one* — even suggested that this was his problem, and that we could help him with medicine. If this problem is so common, why don't they tell every single teacher in the schools how to recognize these children early, and how to help them instead of making matters worse by misunderstanding and sarcasm? Why did the psychologists all blame Steve's behavior on things we were doing wrong? And why didn't any one of our doctors suggest trying the kind of medicine you're going to prescribe? It seems to me someone ought to write a book to tell people about these children so that everyone who deals with them would understand — especially their poor bewildered parents!"

Steve's mother turned abruptly and left me sitting there, wondering how many other children there were just like her youngster — pushed around from agency to agency, embarrassed and frustrated in the classroom, criticized by their teachers and tormented by their classmates, and punished by their parents for misdeeds over which they really had no control. If the report of the National Advisory Committee on Dyslexia and Related Reading Disorders published in 1969 is true — and I believe the statistics are valid — there are eight million children in our schools today who have learning disabilities. Thus this is the most prevalent chronic disorder among all of the children in the country. There are many facts about these youngsters that we do not understand, but we can afford to wait no longer to help them. We must try with the tools we have *now*, even while we wait for research to give us the answers we need for a more thorough understanding. The diagnosis of learning disability is not difficult, and although some of the assumptions we must make about cause and treatment cannot yet be proven beyond doubt, the benefits to the child, when he finally begins to achieve in the classroom and gain the acceptance of his classmates and teachers, need no further confirmation. Investigators may argue about the relative importance of perceptual disorders or motor training, or the value of one remedial method over another, but the "trenches" are in the classroom. Here is where the learning-disabled child must go forth every day to do battle with whatever equipment he has — a square peg trying to fit into a round hole which has been designed for children without his problems, and with whom he must compete every school day. Here in the classroom he succeeds or fails, and if he fails he must usually suffer the consequences of rejection by all those who mean so much to him. And it is in the regular classroom that we must recognize his difficulties and begin our efforts to help him overcome them.

So here is what you asked for, Mrs. B.: a book about children who have trouble learning in school. Other books about learning disabilities are usually written by authorities in all the different fields concerned — vision and hearing, perception and learning, language and behavior — stressing the importance of a multi-disciplinary study of the child and his problems. Most parents, however, have found it difficult to obtain all of these evaluations and services, and then almost impossible to find someone who will assume the responsibility of explaining to them exactly what must be done to help their child. Personal experience with the management of several hundred learning-disabled children has convinced me that the child can be helped most by those closest to him. No program developed on a regional or national basis is going to solve all the problems of every learning-disabled child since each one is different and needs to be treated as an individual. A knowledgeable teacher, concerned parents, and an interested physician comprise the real learning disability team. Together they can try to aid each child according to his own specific needs, helping him reach his true learning potential and keeping him in the mainstream of regular education in his own community where he belongs.

PART ONE

1.

SPECIFIC LEARNING DISABILITY — THE DEVELOPMENT OF A CONCEPT

Because the workings of the human brain and its development through the learning processes are so complicated, the learning-disabled child has been misunderstood by many who have tried to help him. Teachers who are concerned with what to teach and when to teach it, rather than how children learn, cannot understand why all children do not learn equally well; many of these teachers are still not being taught to recognize and understand the problem of learning disability even though it affects four or five children in every classroom. Psychologists recognize that these children have emotional problems, but some still think that they are the *cause* of the child's learning problems, rather than the *result* of them. They still see learning disorders as the result of parental mismanagement, and try to correct them through manipulation of family relationships. And physicians, who hold the key to helping the child's biochemical problem with medication, have, as a rule, been reluctant to become involved in a disorder which seems to be primarily educational, especially since the child reveals none of the usual physical abnormalities the doctor has been trained to recognize.

At one time every school child was considered just as capable of learning as every other child of the same age. The curriculum for each school year was established with the idea of allowing the teacher to consider children as blank slates and inscribe (or have the child learn to inscribe) all the information that was dispensed in exactly the same manner. When a child did not progress at the same rate as his classmates, it was automatically assumed that he was mentally retarded. Classes were developed within the school systems to teach these children using special methods. As it became obvious that a number of intelligent children were being relegated to the category of retarded, other causes were looked for. Perhaps the child could not see or hear well — and this was investigated. If his sensory functions were found unimpaired, consideration was next given to the possibility of factors in the child's environment that might be holding back his learning development, such as emotional disturbances caused by parental mismanagement and family discord, or lack of cultural experiences and a home background that did not afford the right kind of incentive to learn.

But there were many children who had none of these difficulties. When tested they were found to have normal or even superior intelligence; they had adequate vision and hearing; they were emotionally stable; they came from an environment which afforded them proper motivational stimulus for learning, yet they failed to learn from the usual teaching methods. These are the children that we now say have the problem of "specific learning disability." The word "specific" indicates that their difficulty is not due to general external or environmental causes, and "disability" that their problem is distinct from a real deficiency or inability. We must consider uppermost the fact that these children do not have real deficiencies. They *can* learn, once their problems are understood and the proper remedial steps undertaken.

This understanding has been a long time coming, and while many of its aspects are still unclear, specific learning disability is now recognized as one of a group of conditions caused by a disturbed or altered function of the brain, called "dysfunction." Use of the concept of dysfunction (the "dys" meaning defective or faulty, coming from the same root word as the "dis" in disability) was first proposed by Eric Denhoff in 1959 to explain certain disorders which seemed to bear a relationship to one another. These were cerebral palsy, mental retardation, epilepsy, and what was called the "hyperkinetic behavior disorder." All of these syndromes (syndrome refers to a grouping or cluster of symptoms) he considered to be indicative of brain dysfunction. He and his co-workers found that many of the children undergoing treatment at his center for cerebral palsy were not living up to expectations in the classroom, even though their intelligence was tested as being normal and their physical difficulties did not seem to explain their problems. Their teachers reported that the children seemed to be unable to concentrate or follow instructions and showed a number of behavioral disorders usually seen in children considered emotionally immature. Other physicians, interested in finding the cause of these conditions, tried unsuccessfully to locate a specific area of the brain which might be related to each disorder. What they did find was that some children might show symptoms of any or all of these four syndromes. Accordingly, what disorder each child was said to have was determined by its predominant characteristic. If the child could not move or coordinate his muscles properly, he was said to have cerebral palsy; if he had convulsions, he was called epileptic; if his intellectual deficiency predominated, he was called mentally deficient or retarded; and if his behavior was characterized by marked overactivity and impulsivity, he was said to have a hyperkinetic behavior disorder. Later studies revealed that the childhood psychoses could be properly added to this group of disorders, for many of the symptoms appeared to overlap. The child with cerebral palsy might also have convulsions, or he might have the same difficulties in interpreting things that he saw and heard (perceptual disorders) as the hyperkinetic child. Any or all of these children might show emotional immaturity.

Since a number of the children with the more severe disorders had a history of damage to the brain, which had most often occurred during the birth process, it was assumed that the children with less obvious conditions also had brain injury or damage of a lesser degree — that there was a spectrum extending from the more severely involved, who had cerebral palsy, to the less involved, who were said to have minimal brain damage. This term has become deeply imbedded in medical and psychological writing, although efforts are now being taken to accept Dr. Denhoff's suggestion and replace it with the more accurate designation of dysfunction. Learning disability is now recognized to be only one of the indications of the presence of brain dysfunction, albeit a most important one. Careful evaluation of the child will reveal difficulties in either or both of two other areas, activity control and behavior control. It is possible for a child to show evidence of more than one of the disorders of brain dysfunction and, therefore, strict labelling of the child is unwise and often too restrictive. Who knows? In the near future when we understand these children better, all of the terms we now use may become obsolete. This discussion of terms used to describe these children, and the various definitions that have developed, may seem of little consequence, but the deeper one delves into the problem, the more confusing the situation becomes. Parents find that their learning-disabled child may be called "educationally handicapped" (EH) in California, "neurologically handicapped" (NH) in another state and "perceptually handicapped" in yet another. The label may seem unimportant. However, in order to qualify for aid from special funds appropriated by the legislatures of the various states to provide special educational facilities, the child's problem must be adjusted to fit the nomenclature used by the local program if he is to get help. A special task force was appointed by the Easter Seal Research Foundation and the National Institute of Neurological Diseases and Blindness of the Public Health Service to review the thirty-eight terms used to describe the basic disorder and try to create some order from all the semantic confusion. They found one large group of expressions being applied to the supposed cause of the disturbances ("organic brain disease," "minimal brain damage," and so forth) while the other group described the effects of these conditions as observed in the child's distorted behavior and performance ("hyperkinetic behavior syndrome," "dyslexia," "perceptual cripple," and so forth). Neither group covered the subject in a manner broad enough to include all the children and all the various aspects of the difficulties encountered, and the old arguments of heredity vs. environment added further confusion. The Task Force finally reached agreement and published their study in 1966 as Public Health Service Publication No. 1415 (NINDB Monograph No. 3) entitled "Minimal Brain Dysfunction in Children," covering terminology and identification. Task Force Two covered the educational, medical and health related services (Public Health Service Publication No. 2015, 1969) and a review of the research in the field by Task Force Three, entitled "Central Processing Dysfunctions in Children," was published as NINDS Monograph No. 3.

This latter terminology — central processing dysfunction — is a more accurate description of the real problem, but "minimal brain dysfunction" is the designation which workers in the medical, psychological and educational professions are now accepting. My only objection to it is to the connotation of the adjective "minimal" which might be thought to indicate "trivial," for there is certainly nothing trivial about the impact this condition has upon the child's developing personality. A better adjective would have been "subtle" since the clinical findings are often so elusive and confusing; but since it has taken so long to reach an agreement, let us accept the term minimal brain dysfunction without any further argument. For the sake of brevity I shall occasionally use the abbreviations MBD when minimal brain dysfunction is intended, SLD for a specific learning disability, and LD for learning-disabled.

Figure 1 shows the relationship of MBD and SLD to

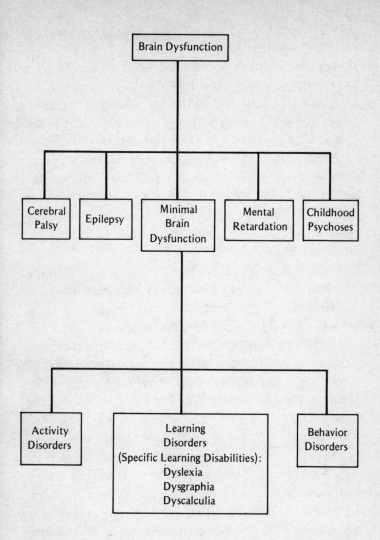

Figure 1. The Family Tree of Specific Learning Disabilities

these other disorders in graphic form. This should serve as a reminder that specific learning disability is but one symptom of a complex, and as yet incompletely understood, group of disorders that are probably interrelated through the chemicals involved in the finer coordinated functions of the brain and nervous system. Dyslexia (difficulty with reading), dyscalculia (difficulty with mathematics) and dysgraphia (difficulty with writing) are the individual symptoms of the basic underlying disorder, indicating the specific educational problem affecting the child with SLD.

As our knowledge of children with SLD expanded, certain characteristics became evident which have helped us understand their problems more clearly. Those first teachers who helped Dr. Denhoff with his children had made the very important observation that the children seemed to function in a very immature manner. Since those early days, parents and teachers have echoed these same sentiments, making it evident that, if we are to understand the basic difficulty, we will have to discover why these children have not matured as readily as other children.

Through the pioneering efforts of Arnold Gesell, we have been furnished with a remarkable set of observations concerning a child's climb up the developmental ladder: how most children are sitting by six to eight months of age, standing by eleven to fourteen months, and walking without help between twelve and eighteen months. At the same time the developing child is exploring his environment by touching, grasping, putting things to his face and in his mouth, and learning, sometimes to his discomfort, that there are differences in texture, taste and temperature. As his activity progresses, he also learns to use language, first with a single "coo," then babbling single sounds, finally progressing to single words to which he begins to attach meaning, until by two to two-and-a-half years of age he is able to communicate in short sentences.

Although much of a child's progress is innate, the environment can exert a favorable or an adverse influence on him, depending upon the kinds of opportunities and experiences he encounters. But even more important is the feedback which the child experiences from within himself and from those about him. One successful step encourages another, then another, building confidence as well as establishing patterns to be used later, either to repeat the same act or to use in a new situation. And in speech, the importance of feedback is paramount, for communication is a two-way street. The child soon learns he can influence his listener by what he says, and he builds up his use of speech from what he hears in response. A smile from Mother and her favorable reply will encourage him to try new words and to watch for their effects.

Unless some mishap occurs to interfere with his progress, the child continues to move along toward a state of developmental maturity usually reached by the age of six. By this time he has explored his own body, and used his command of speech in becoming aware of his body parts and their names and locations. Through moving his body he becomes aware of his location in the physical world and can soon judge distances and the lapse of time, which are related spatial concepts. Most important of all, when he reaches developmental maturity, he is able to achieve a certain measure of self-control. He no longer needs to be in constant motion, and can remain quiet sufficiently long enough to concentrate on specific matters which require his attention. He can control his speech so that he is able to await his turn in the give-and-take of proper social conversation. He is able to move his legs, arms, hands and fingers in the way he wishes in co-ordinated activities, and can use his eyes to help direct them readily toward a desired object. He has developed a certain amount of skill with one hand which he prefers to use for the performance of more complicated acts. Along with these controls of his activity he has also developed the ability to regulate his behavior in a manner acceptable to those about him. He no longer cries as readily, is not as impulsive and can postpone the gratification of his wishes. He will concentrate on one task at a time and see it through to completion, or leave it when directed to attend another. He remembers instructions and follows directions in a generally organized manner, and is able to build upon his previous experience and knowledge to approach the solution of new problems.

This then is the child who has attained developmental maturity, and, while there is wide variation in the attainment of all these various attributes, we can generally say that they are expected to be present in the child before he enters regular school, which is usually at the age of six. We can assume that the child who shows these characteristics has begun life with a properly built brain and nervous system with correct chemical functions, that he has been given the opportunity to build experiences to enhance his progress, and that with the right amount of

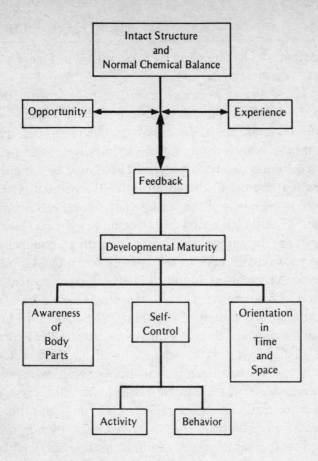

Figure 2. Normal Developmental Maturity

The child born with an intact nervous system having a normal structure and correct chemical functions will progress to maturity by virtue of his innate drive to do so. He will explore his environment, achieving progressive levels of learning by building upon previous experiences, as long as he is given sufficient opportunity to do so. His advancement is influenced by the feedback which he receives from every successful accomplishment, which encourages him to new and more varied successes. He will thus attain, at about the age of six, a level of developmental maturity at which he can readily identify the parts of his body, is firmly established as to time and space, and can maintain reasonable self-control over his activity and behavior.

feedback he has followed the path shown in Figure 2 to reach developmental maturity.

The desire to attain maturity is a basic drive within every child and, when he fails to achieve it properly, we can be certain something is wrong. The brain itself may not have been formed properly, or may have been damaged during the birth process. There may be some inherited disorder in the chemistry of the nervous system seen in members of the same family. Illness or injury in early life may have produced structural or chemical damage even though the child began life with an unimpaired nervous system. Lack of opportunity to express himself, or an environment in which the necessary experiences are too few, can limit the child's progress, and his own distorted impressions of the things that happen to him can all combine to keep him from reaching the desired level. Figure 3 outlines how any or all of these various factors can retard the rate of maturing, resulting in what some observers have called a "developmental lag." Whatever the case, the child so afflicted will show the altered awareness of his body parts, confused orientation in time and space, and poor self-control of his activities and behavior now considered to be the manifestations of minimal brain dysfunction. With this basic background we can proceed to see how to recognize the child with minimal brain dysfunction and, most important of all, how to help him cope with his problems in the classroom. We call these problems specific learning disabilities.

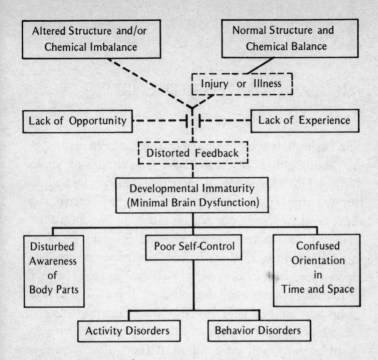

Figure 3. Abnormal Development in Minimal Brain Dysfunction

When a child is born with a structural defect in his nervous system or has inherited a chemical imbalance which affects its proper function, or when he sustains damage from illness or injury to a normal nervous system, he does not progress to maturity in the same manner as an undamaged child. He does not correctly process the sensory information coming to him from his own body and from the world about him, thus disturbing the build-up of successful experiences and feedback necessary for satisfactory development. If those about him do not reinforce his efforts by encouragement and approval, he will lack sufficient motivation to overcome the obstacles in his path toward developmental maturity.

The child who remains immature for whatever reasons has a disturbed awareness of his body parts, is confused about time and space relationships, and shows poor control over his activity and behavior. These deficiencies leave him ill-equipped to profit from regular classroom instruction and compete with other children who do not have the same difficulties.

2.

THE LEARNING-DISABLED CHILD

The basic underlying disorder of the children with specific learning disability that I have seen is minimal brain dysfunction. The nature of their problems is revealed by the way they act and talk, by the way they behave and think, and by their poor performance in the classroom. Their failure to reach the expected level of developmental maturity, as described in the previous chapter, leaves them with inadequate self-control so that they are unable to compete with the other children of their age group who do not have this disorder. Figure 4 lists the symptoms most often reported by the parents and teachers of learning-disabled children. Although each child is an individual who may respond to his disorder in his own way, there are enough similarities weaving themselves into recognizable patterns to allow us to identify these youngsters with a reasonable degree of accuracy. Once the true nature of the difficulties is understood, it is possible to develop a plan to assist each child to overcome his particular handicap so that he is better able to continue with his classmates in the regular school routine.

DISORDERS OF ACTIVITY

Hyperactivity

The most noticeable characteristic of the child with minimal brain dysfunction and specific learning disabilities, and the one which annoys parents and teachers most, is overactivity. The child never seems able to sit still, is constantly getting up and down, roaming about from place to place, handling everything in sight, knocking over objects and stumbling into those around him, and keeping everyone in a constant state of turmoil. He exhausts everyone who tries to watch him or keep up with him, yet he never seems to run out of energy. As one father commented to me, "This kid's carburetor must be turned up way too high; he never stops!"

Even when quite young the hyperactive child is apt to pull away from anyone trying to care for him and dart into traffic or other hazards with total disregard for bodily harm. He is constantly exploring, climbing, and falling. His frequent visits to the emergency room for repair of lacerations and setting of broken bones earn him the reputation of being accident-prone. As he gets older, his total overactivity may decrease somewhat, but he still wriggles and fidgets, and seems never to be at complete rest, giving the impression that he is a nervous child. In the classroom he shuffles his feet, drums his fingers on the desk, hums to himself, is up and down to sharpen his pencil and bumps into the child next to him on the way back to his desk. With increasing age the hyperactivity decreases and the behavioral and academic difficulties become matters of greater concern.

Another name for the overactive child is hyperkinetic. When I explained to one mother that this term was derived from two Greek words — "hyper" meaning excess of and "kinesis" referring to activity — she readily agreed that it was most appropriate for her child. " 'Excess' is his middle name," she said. "Everything about him is excess. He's been that way ever since he got here. He screamed every night from the time we brought him home from the hospital. He had horrible colic and it seemed we were changing his formula every other week. He was sitting alone by four months, and when he was ten months old he took off from his crib running at full speed and he hasn't stopped since. You know — I can remember him kicking me more than my other children before he was even born!"

Not every mother gives such a graphic description of her child and his problems. If the hyperactive youngster is an only child, his mother may be unable to compare him with others, and, feeling that activity is a characteristic of all small children, may not think that anything is wrong. But when her child is compelled to sit still in the classroom along with other children of his own age, it soon becomes evident that something is wrong. The teacher often observes that the child's basic problem is a lack of self-control, and may feel that he just hasn't been taught this by his mother, whom she may feel has overprotected or spoiled him. Kindly in-laws and neighbors may contribute the same opinion, and even his own father may express the idea that "there's nothing wrong with this kid that a good licking wouldn't cure." Beating after beating may be administered without any improvement, seeming to confirm the suspicion that the child has been just "spoiled rotten." The bewildered mother is unable to explain to herself what she has done to produce the problem and may indeed be forced to overprotect her child from those who would continue punishing him for

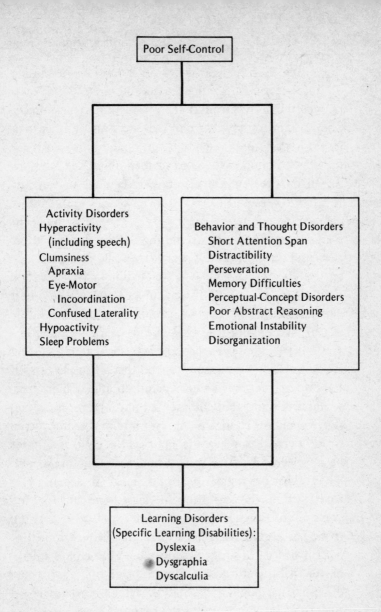

Figure 4. Symptoms of the Child with Specific Learning Disabilities

something that she feels is not his fault. This just brings on more comments about "smother love" and compounds the guilt already built up in the mother's mind. She remembers how her child, even as a tiny infant, rejected her attempts to cuddle and fondle him, and if she has studied child psychology or read about the latest research on the importance of body contact in early infancy, she is bound to feel that her child's problems are a reflection of her inadequacies as a mother. Since he seems to need to touch everything that attracts his attention and is particularly prone to cling to people, he creates the impression that he requires more affection than other children. This convinces some of the adults who deal with him that his parents must be cold and rejecting. Meanwhile the child becomes more and more aware that he is unacceptable to his parents, to his teacher, and to his classmates, and this feeling lowers his self-esteem and adds to his frustration and unhappiness.

Another trait often commented upon by those around the hyperactive child is his incessant talking. Almost continually verbalizing, even to himself, the child soon finds he is rejected by others who find this trait obnoxious. The teacher has a great deal of difficulty in keeping him from continually disrupting the classroom, since he answers out of turn and frequently interrupts others. Again, if she has decided that her classroom will be a model of perfect decorum, she will soon report the child's misbehavior in little notes sent home, suggesting that firmer discipline be applied or that the child be deprived of something until he learns better manners.

Because hyperactivity is considered normal in the small child, and because what may seem to be overactivity to one observer may not be as noticeable to another, it is often difficult to draw a line and state at which age or at what level overactivity should be considered abnormal. Attempts have been made to measure activity scientifically by using motion pictures taken through a two-way glass or by placing a pedometer, like a watch, on the wrist of the child to calculate his total daily movements. Competent teachers can give a reliable report by comparing the learning-disabled child with the rest of his classmates. However, there is some danger in allowing an observer with a low rate of tolerance for annoyance to be the judge, or to use hyperactivity as the sole criterion for considering the child to have minimal brain dysfunction. Careful examination will usually disclose some of the other findings consistent with MBD, such as confusion about body parts, attention-span and memory deficits, and instability of emotional control. Not all hyperactive children are doomed to classroom failure, and those who can figure out a way to overcome this difficulty may actually be able to go on to outstanding academic careers.

Clumsiness

Another trait frequently found in children with minimal brain dysfunction is clumsiness. The child is noted to be awkward at an early age, and, instead of developing a smooth and graceful flow of muscular coordination, he stumbles and falls a great deal and cannot keep up with the other children in his neighborhood. He has trouble learning to ride a tricycle or bicycle and has great difficulty in dressing himself, especially in tying his shoes. This lack of skill prolongs his dependence upon his parents and hinders his development of self-reliance. Inability to do purposeful acts requiring skilled use of the hands and fingers is called "apraxia," a difficulty that becomes particularly incapacitating when the child begins to use crayons and pencils. For example, in kindergarten when he tries to color pictures, he has trouble staying within the lines and boundaries, and he cannot copy geometrical forms such as a circle, square or triangle. When he enters the first grade his awkward grasp of the pencil makes handwriting a real chore. This characteristic is considered a key factor in alerting the teacher to detect a learning-disabled child early in his school career.

Along with difficulties in the use of his fingers and hands (also called fine motor incoordination), and awkwardness in moving his arms and legs (gross motor incoordination), the MBD child shows an imbalance in the manner in which his eyes move. The eye muscles show jerky action as the child attempts to track the course of a moving light or other object. This imbalance, manifesting itself in frequent hesitations and backtracking, interferes with his ability to follow the directions of the words on the printed page from left to right in a smooth manner. Further evidence of the difficulty is shown when the child attempts to copy figures or words, so that he is said to have poor eye-hand or faulty visual-motor coordination.

He may show jerky, irregular movements when asked to turn his hands over and back, and may even have a noticeable tremor when holding his arms straight out from his body. He is often unable to hop on one foot, or walk a straight line, or alternate between running and skipping. He may show a preference for using his right hand to throw, his left foot to kick, and his left eye to sight (mixed laterality), and he frequently finds it impossible to close one eye at a time, even though he appears skilled in many other acts.

Not every LD child is clumsy; in fact some are outstanding athletes and can compensate for their classroom inadequacies by excelling in sports. Unfortunately, they often still encounter difficulties since they must maintain a certain grade average to participate in athletics, and some find their learning disability an annoying impediment to their physical achievement. Interestingly enough, some of the fathers of my LD children readily admit that they themselves would have never made it through high school or college were it not for their physical prowess and the academic doors thus opened to them.

Hypoactivity

There is another group of learning-disabled children who appear to be the exact opposite of the hyperactive children. They sit quietly in the back of the classroom, creating no disturbance and causing the teacher to comment on how well behaved they are. The disability of these hypoactive children is difficult to detect because of its subtle nature and because so many observers have so long considered hyperactivity to be an essential component of the learning disability pattern. But the competent teacher will notice that these children do not live up to expectation in academic performance. They rarely volunteer to participate in classroom discussion, and seem to be trying to keep from being noticed in order to avoid the humiliation that comes with exposure of their inadequacies. Because they are not behavior problems in the classroom, these children may be so successful in concealing their difficulty that they receive automatic "social" promotion year after year, and may reach the high school level before the real nature of their problem is discovered. They are most often clumsy and insecure, and on the playground at school can usually be found off by themselves. Teachers and classmates often refer to them as "loners." Future investigations may find that this group comprises a much larger segment of our learning-disabled population than is now realized.

Sleep Problems

Another common complaint which parents report concerning children with MBD is that they have abnormal sleep patterns. Many have told of the difficulty they have with their child, even at a very early age, in getting him to sleep and keeping him in bed through the night. Many of these children are wanderers, being up and about the house at all hours; others are rollers and tossers, ending up on the floor with the bedclothes wrapped around them. Frequently parents say that their children cry out in their sleep, or grind their teeth, or wake up an hour or so after falling asleep and are unable to go back to sleep. Others are just the opposite: once they get to sleep they sleep so deeply that it is almost impossible to arouse them with anything short of physical force. Many of these very deep sleepers continue to wet the bed long beyond the usual age — another source of embarrassment and lowered self-opinion, especially if the child is made to feel that these mishaps are all his fault.

DISORDERS OF BEHAVIOR AND THOUGHT

Short Attention Span (Distractibility)

The almost universal complaint of parent and teacher alike about the learning-disabled child is his short attention span. He seems totally unable to concentrate and is readily distracted, changing from one activity or subject to another without ever completing the task at hand. Because of his distractibility he cannot organize his work or follow any sequence of order directed toward a definite goal. He does only part of his assignments and homework, and rarely finishes an examination; the ones that he does complete he usually rushes through and seldom goes back to correct his frequent errors. He seems totally unaware of these deficiencies, and no matter how many F's or Incompletes he receives, or how many notes are sent home to his parents (a good number of which never seem to reach their goal!) the pattern goes on and on. He is frequently accused of being a day-dreamer, although many times he may be hearing everything that is taking place while appearing inattentive. One mother complained to me, "He seems to have a built-in hearing aid that he can just turn on and off at will." Because of this trait he may seem to be willfully disobedient and is frequently punished for it, which does not really improve the situation.

Perseveration

With all his distractibility and attention difficulties, the LD child will sometimes become so absorbed in doing something in which he is interested that he will spend hours deeply involved and nothing short of force can tear him away. This characteristic has been called "perseveration." It seems to be quite a paradox in behavior until it is noted that the child persists in an activity because he has at last found something he can do, something in which he can succeed, and something in which he is comfortable. Teachers have found this attribute most disconcerting in the classroom, for, when it is time to put away one text and go on to another subject, the teacher cannot tolerate the child's inability to let go and start something else. Parents who note this characteristic at home are inclined to describe their child as strong willed or bullheaded.

Memory Difficulties

The short attention span of the LD child is related to another of his learning problems, memory deficits. When he is given a series of instructions to follow, he seems unable to remember their sequence. His mother may meet him at the back door with the admonitions: "Don't forget to wipe your feet, go hang up your jacket in the front closet, then wash your hands for dinner, be sure to wipe your hands on the green towel and don't come to the table without combing your hair." Much to her dismay she may later find her child still standing at the back door trying to recall the first step that he was supposed to take. In the classroom this sequential memory deficit is disastrous, as can well be imagined. The teacher says, "Now, children, the assignment for tomorrow is to read Chapter Five in your text, answer the first six questions at the bottom of page thirty-two, then outline the first paragraph in Section Three of your work-book." When the LD child arrives home and is asked about homework he is apt to reply that none was assigned, rather than admit that he just cannot remember. And he would prefer to face the fury of his teacher the next day and receive a zero rather than reveal his deficiency before his classmates! Since many teachers will interpret this as an expression of lack of interest, laziness, or worse, the child may wind up with yet another note home to his parents with the suggestion that they take away some of their child's privileges, or apply more pressure. And just to be sure that they do, the teacher may double the amount of homework!

One of the more puzzling aspects of the memory problems of the LD child is the inconsistency of his performance. One day he seems to be able to remember everything taught him, the next day he has forgotten everything. The child may be able to recite an entire assignment without error on the night before a test, then fail miserably the next day. Unless inconsistency of performance is recognized as a characteristic trait of specific learning disability, it may be felt to indicate lack of interest or poor motivation for success, and for this the parents usually get blamed once again.

Perceptual-Concept Disorders

Among the various disorders in the thought processes of the child with MBD, those which interfere with his ability to properly interpret and utilize the information he receives has the greatest effect on his ability to learn. These disorders of perception involve primarily the fields of visual and auditory discrimination and processing, and their significance is readily appreciated when we note how frequently the term perceptually handicapped is used as a synonym for learning-disabled.

Even though he has no true visual problem in terms of refractive error, or clarity of the visual image, the MBD child may have difficulty in recognizing what he sees as being similar to or different from something he has seen before. He may be unable to distinguish between shapes and forms or between objects which resemble one another; he may find it impossible to combine several visual stimuli into a usable whole; and he may not easily be able to see how an object resembles other familiar objects or remember and recall visual images. Nearly every one of us has experienced visual perceptual difficulties, such as the false appearance of water on the highway when driving on a sunny day, but experience reminds us that this is just an illusion. The child with MBD makes repeated visual errors, including reversals of letters and whole words, and seems unaware of his problem since he makes the same mistakes over and over. His visual perceptual distortion may be increased by his spatial confusion and eye-motor incoordination which prevent him from scanning objects carefully for comparison, or from progressing smoothly from left to right across the printed page as he must do in learning to read.

Auditory perceptual disorders include problems in discriminating sounds, comparing and associating them with other sounds, and making the necessary sound-and-sight blendings so essential to the ability to read. Distortions in hearing are even more dependent upon experience than are visual errors, and some of the auditory imperceptions made by young children turn out to be quite amusing. There is the case of the three-year-old from Brooklyn who recited the Lord's Prayer: "Lead me not to Penn Station." Sound-alikes may bother everyone but the individual with learning disability has little appreciation for that lowest form of humor, the pun. ("It's not the school I dislike, it's the principal of the thing.")

Both visual and auditory perception begin with the reception of sensory stimuli and this is directly dependent upon the ability of the child to pay attention. The attention-span deficit so common to MBD thus impairs the perceptual process at its very start. Many investigators are now suggesting that the true basis of learning disorders is this lack of attention at the beginning of the act of perception and processing of information. They suggest that steps taken to improve the attention span hold out the greatest hope for improving the learning disorder.

By failing to utilize visual and auditory information properly, the learning-disabled child finds himself unable to make the proper judgments, comparisons and generalizations necessary for establishing concepts such as size, distance, direction, weight and other categories important in the learning process. His faulty interpretations may carry over into social situations where his distorted perceptions may lead him to feel that he is being misunderstood and treated unfairly, that everyone is against him, and that he is always being made to carry the blame for the wrongs that others do.

Disturbances frequently noted in the MBD child are confusion about space and time and faulty identification of body parts. He has difficulty in understanding the differences between up and down, front and back, above and beneath, and especially between left and right (confused laterality). Since reading and writing depend so much upon a smooth left-to-right progression, these problems significantly hinder the learning-disabled child's progress in the classroom. The passage of time is closely related to spatial concepts, so many of the LD children have an unusual amount of difficulty in learning to tell time and in understanding the numerical concepts involved in handling money or in other mathematical tasks. This spatial confusion carries over to interfere with the child's ability to name his body parts and correctly tell their location when moved. If asked to place his right heel on his left knee while lying down, he may have to sit up to see where they are before moving them, and even with this visual reinforcement he may have difficulty in figuring out what is asked of him or how to move to comply with the direction. With his eyes closed, the LD child will have difficulty in identifying individual toes when they are touched, and may be confused about the directions in which they are moved. Similar difficulties are reported about tests involving the fingers (finger agnosia), and in correct interpretation when the face and hand are touched simultaneously (tactile discrimination) or when figures are drawn across the skin (graphesthesia).

Another problem that has been reported concerning the LD child is his difficulty in separating one object from another in a grouping, or in distinguishing an object that should be especially noted from the general background — this is called the figure-ground disturbance. All of us speak of occasionally not being able to tell the forest for the trees, or vice-versa, and in this kind of discrimination the LD child is really handicapped. When he encounters a picture with many different objects of various shapes, he becomes confused and often misses the entire idea of the subject being portrayed. This disability occurs not only when he sorts out the objects that he sees, but also when he tries to listen while many things are going on at once. He is unable to follow his teacher's voice when it gets mixed in with the sniffling of the child behind him or footsteps in the hall outside. (In adult life we call this the cocktail party syndrome.) These problems in visual and auditory discrimination are associated with the attention-span deficiency and the distractibility previously mentioned as important factors in learning disabilities.

Poor Abstract Reasoning

An additional disturbance in the thought process of the LD child, which is apparently related to immaturity, is his inability to progress from concrete to abstract thinking. Everything for the child is in the here and now. He seems unable to project into the future, and cannot grasp the fact that how he acts in his relationships with other people will affect how they will subsequently treat him. He is very open and naive, and the more subtle shades of meaning seem to elude him. He may repeatedly demand to have things explained to him, for he just cannot seem to "catch on" as readily as other children. Yet in the classroom he often becomes ashamed of his inadequacy and rarely will raise his hand when his teacher asks if anyone doesn't understand. He would prefer to struggle on rather than risk the laughter and ridicule of his classmates. (Teachers are now even recognizing this trait in students who have progressed as far as medical school!) His inability to figure things out and project his thinking into the future can hound a person with a learning disability even into adult life, and will interfere with his acceptance and the impression he will make on his superiors. Remember the story of the great architect, Sir Christopher Wren, who came upon three workmen participating in the construction of St. Paul's in London? He asked each man what he was doing. The first said he was putting one brick on top of the other, the second replied that he was making so many shillings a day for his work, while the third replied that he was building a great cathedral. I'm afraid that our LD child could never visualize the result of his labors in the way the third man did.

Emotional Instability (Impulsivity; Inconsistency)

The behavior of every child with MBD and subsequent SLD is characterized by the most obvious sign of his developmental immaturity — poor emotional control and stability. He cries more readily than other children, is easily frustrated and acts impulsively, with little apparent concern for the consequences of what he does to others. He seems crushed and overwhelmed whenever corrected or punished for his misbehavior. Every small upset becomes a major catastrophe and relatively trivial things which do not bother his siblings or classmates seem to totally dismantle him. This extreme sensitivity caused one mother to say, "Things just seem to 'bug' him a lot more than they do my other children." Because of his immature actions the LD child is often suspected of merely trying to attract attention. His increased demands on his parents and teachers usually bring him more scolding and punishment, and he is told, "Big boys don't act that way." How frustrating it must be for these children to be constantly reminded of their defect and to see their lack of acceptance by their parents, teachers, and classmates! There is in every child a basic innate drive toward growth and maturity and the hindrance caused by minimal brain dysfunction disrupts this natural sequence of events and blocks the development of self-reliance and self-esteem. Rejection by his peers further compounds the emotional drain to which the learning-disabled child is daily subjected.

He desperately wants to be accepted and become a part of the group. He may even steal money from his parents or articles from stores which he will offer to others in his efforts to please. But his behavior is often so obnoxious that he is rarely tolerated, and, children being as frank (or as cruel) as they are, are not reluctant to let him know what they think of him. This naturally produces the expected effect. The child so treated either retreats further into his shell, becoming ready game for his tormentors, or strikes back at a situation which he finds intolerable. Fights on the playground are followed by mishaps in the hallway and finally in the classroom. Visits to the principal's office are then succeeded by suspension and finally expulsion. This convinces the child with MBD that what he has believed all along is true — no one really cares about him and everyone is against him. How many of us would act differently under the same circumstances?

Another perplexing feature of the behavior of the MBD child is inconsistency. Years ago a mother told me "You know, some days there's a cloud between my child and me, and on other days the sun is shining brightly." I didn't know then what she meant, but I do now. This is an almost constant complaint of those who try to understand the child with minimal brain dysfunction and learning disabilities, and while I can't explain it, this observation is so frequently made that it must be mentioned. You may try to blame this variability on the weather, humidity, or other atmospheric conditions, but it is exasperating to parent and teacher alike to encounter those bad days when it is impossible for the child to get anything done. All of us have days when things seem to go wrong, when we feel we must have gotten up on the wrong side of the bed, but for the learning-disabled child the whole world is turned upside down on these days.

Teachers and parents who are unaware of this characteristic cannot understand the reason. If a child was able to do a certain lesson well on one day, why does he do so dismally on another? It is one of the unexplained burdens that we simply must learn to live with in our present state of knowledge (or ignorance) and we should stop punishing these children for things that are not really their fault.

Disorganization

The combined effect of these disturbed thought processes in the learning-disabled child is a general disorganization in the way he approaches tasks and attempts to solve problems. He rarely completes an assignment or finishes an examination, and doesn't seem able to plan ahead to carry out any particular obligation to its completion. One parent told me how she would go over an assignment with her child the night before an examination, satisfied that he knew all the answers, only to be disappointed the next day by another F. When she would examine the test paper she would find that the first five or six questions had been answered fairly well, but the rest of the paper was blank. When asked what had happened, her child would answer, "The bell rang." She could never get him to realize that if there were ten questions on the exam and sixty minutes in the hour, he would have to allow five to six minutes to each question and pace himself accordingly. This disorganized behavior is a characteristic seen in almost everything the LD child undertakes. The teacher who does not recognize this as a symptom of MBD will continue to hound the child, insisting he could do better if he would just try harder or if he were really interested in his school work.

LEARNING DISORDERS
(SPECIFIC LEARNING DISABILITIES)

Dyslexia

This single word has caused more controversy than any other in the whole field of learning disabilities, and page after page has been written trying to define what it means. For our purposes let's agree that it means trouble with reading, and then try to understand why an intelligent, well-motivated child simply cannot learn to decipher the significance of what the printed word is supposed to represent as readily as his classmates. He may be able to see the printed word "church" — he may even be able to spell out each letter, "c-h-u-r-c-h," and say "church" — but he doesn't see in his mind's eye the building with a steeple that these letters are supposed to symbolize. Often when he attempts to read, he reverses words saying "was" instead of "saw," "tap" instead of "pat." Many times he will substitute a different word, or will omit an entire word or phrase. Since the words themselves escape him individually, he may try to follow the general meaning of the entire sentence and read "mother" instead of "parent." He may seem to be able to handle the larger words better than the short ones, such as "the," "an," "it." His confusion may carry over into his speech, and he often has a great deal of difficulty in coming up with the correct name for a specific object. He will say "the thing you cook on" or "the thing you fix supper on" instead of being able to state "stove" or "oven." These peculiar characteristics — anomia, substitutions, reversals and confusion of symbolic meanings (which the pioneer Samuel Orton called "strephosymbolia," meaning twisted symbols) are indicative of the specific nature of the dyslexic child's problems and should clarify the differences between his reading difficulties and those of the child with retardation, emotional disturbance, or environmental deprivation.

Since reading is such an important avenue toward the acquisition of knowledge, failure to learn to read is undoubtedly the most disabling handicap that any schoolchild could have. Unable to understand and keep up with his lessons, the dyslexic child watches in dismay as his classmates with apparent ease master the skills needed for reading. He begins to wonder what is wrong with himself, and soon concludes that he must be retarded or stupid. Rather than reveal this humiliating fact to his teacher or his classmates, he may attempt to conceal his problem by bluffing his way along, and if he has a skilled ear and good memory he may succeed for quite a while, failing only when the material becomes too difficult by about the third or fourth grade. One mother told me she just could not believe it when her child's teacher said her daughter was having trouble with reading. "Every day," she said, "I would pick up Jane at school and bring her home, and we would sit down and go through her reading together. Then one day we had to go to town shopping right after school and didn't get home until just before dinner. I told Jane to sit in the kitchen and read to me while I was cooking. She began to read while I worked at the stove with my back turned. She was doing fine until I turned around and saw she had the book upside down! She must have memorized it all!" If unable to hide his ineptness the child may attempt to attain acceptance from his classmates by becoming the class clown (one mother told me, "My boy was the Red Skelton of the third grade"), or he may pretend to be totally disinterested or bored with everything that goes on in the classroom. This attitude is annoying and disconcerting to the teacher, but if she is astute it should alert her to the possibility that her pupil's real problem is a learning disability.

Dyslexia is far from a rare disorder. A number of studies indicate that nearly thirty percent of all our sixth grade students are reading at a level two grades or more below their class placement. Unfortunately at the present time in many school systems a child is not considered to have a reading disability until he is two grades behind, which means he is automatically subjected to at least three or four years of frustration before his problem is even discovered. Dyslexia is a complex problem. When the entire school population is studied, other factors may be discovered, but the importance of minimal brain dysfunction as a causative factor is increasingly being recognized.

Not every LD child has dyslexia, so we miss a number of these children if we limit our attention exclusively to the dyslexic group. Difficulty with reading is only one symptom, albeit an important one, of the overall complex, and its handling must take into account the whole picture of minimal brain dysfunction. Concentration on just this one symptom has caused much of the confusion that exists today in many of the studies about this problem. Realization that dyslexia, as seen in the LD child, is not an isolated disorder or specific disease but just one of the manifestations of MBD should place it in its proper perspective.

The overall importance of dyslexia has many significant ramifications. All of us esteem highly the individual who is well-read, and the caliber of an educational institution is felt to be closely related to the number of volumes in its library. The child who experiences difficulty in understanding what books are trying to say, or who cannot easily go and look things up when he needs more information about a subject, soon falls behind not only in classroom performance but also, and even more importantly, in self-esteem. Even if he is able to survive his basic education, as he grows older he finds that his inability to read shuts the door on many opportunities for advanced education and job placements. And if he cannot survive even basic education, the correlation between dyslexia as a leading cause of young people dropping out of school and their subsequent delinquency is all too well demonstrated, and this has been amply documented in reports.

We will discuss this important facet of learning disability in much greater detail in the later chapters.

Dysgraphia

Equally disturbing as the inability to learn to read is the difficulty that the learning-disabled child encounters when he begins to learn to write. The same reversals that plague him in reading show up in his handwriting, and he often turns his letters and numbers completely around so that they are mirror-images of the correct ones. And the general disorganization that characterizes his entire school work becomes most obvious when he attempts to put his thoughts down on paper. There is an overall sloppiness about his work that is appalling to his teacher and embarrassing to the pupil himself. He seems unaware when he is approaching the edge of the paper and tends to break up his words with no feeling for their proper division. Without guide lines, his writing wanders up and down the page and the overall result is often almost totally illegible.

But the dysgraphic child can tell you verbally what he is trying to say, and this disparity between having the knowledge and not being able to put it down on paper must be a most frustrating experience. In our present school system, knowledge is measured by how well a child performs on his tests, most of which are written, and his grades soon document his inabilities in this area.

Most children who have problems with writing also have difficulty with spelling. Many tend to spell each word as it sounds to them. Since so many teachers feel duty-bound to take points off a grade for misspelled words, the disaster is compounded. As with other aspects of their inept school performance, many children would prefer to turn in a blank paper and suffer the consequences rather than reveal their difficulty and invite ridicule and embarrassment.

Many books have been written about dyslexia, as if reading problems were the only difficulties that the LD child faced, but I feel this problem with writing which interferes so much with the expression of what has been learned is of equal if not greater importance. Many children who are not succeeding in school may not really have a *learning* disability but a *performance* disability in putting their knowledge down on paper. We will also go into this more thoroughly in future chapters.

Dyscalculia

Since mathematics is a communicating skill based on the relationships of abstract symbols, it is easy to understand why a number of children with learning disabilities find arithmetic and other phases of math extremely difficult. Some may be able to handle the 2 + 2 and 5 + 5 level, but when the problems begin to say, "Farmer Brown had three chickens, two cows, and one duck, how many animals did he have altogether?" their inability to visualize the abstract blocks their progress. Others encounter the same difficulty in organization that they have with their handwriting, so their numerical columns tend to wander all over the paper. Often in the early stages they tend to write numbers in reverse just as they do letters. They find it almost impossible to figure out the value of money, so frequently come home with the incorrect amount of change when sent to the store. This can arouse the ire of their parents, who accuse them of being careless or inattentive, further straining the family relationships. They also have a great deal of difficulty in learning to tell time, and the significance of the passage of time escapes them. As a result they are not very punctual about being at places on time and may stay out playing for hours without coming home. The result usually is: "Don't tell me — you weren't paying attention again!"

Not every LD child encounters problems in math; in fact some find this their one experience with academic success. In a school system which fails to take into account individual differences in learning skills, and has a fixed curriculum for all, the learning-disabled child is penalized either way. If he fails in math alone, he is often forced to repeat the entire grade because of this one difficulty, while if he excels in math, but fails reading, he is also held back. In either case he is frustrated and becomes bored by unnecessary repetition, losing what incentive he may have previously had for learning.

Difficulty with mathematics has not received the amount of publicity that dyslexia has, and is not devastating in its consequences as illiteracy may be, but it can be a source of bewilderment and humiliation to a sensitive child who wonders why he does so poorly in this one subject. Here again an alert teacher who is aware of the problems of the learning-disabled child can do much to tide him through difficult times.

3.

WHY STEVE REALLY CAN'T READ

With the background that we have now established to help us understand why Steve, the young man mentioned earlier, has been acting the way he has, let us now approach the most important aspect of his learning disability, his difficulty with reading. Learning in our school system is closely related to reading; in fact, some observers are inclined to consider reading disability the same as learning disability. Most of the "achievement" tests, by which school progress is judged, lean heavily upon reading ability, and reading difficulties are often the primary reason for failure and grade retention. Since we have now determined that dyslexia is not a disease that can be prevented like measles or treated like scarlet fever, but is a complicated and confusing symptom of an even more complicated and confusing syndrome, let's look at how the LD child performs in the classroom and decide how to help him.

Reading is the process of interpreting the ideas or concepts that printed or written symbols are intended to represent. These symbols (letters) are grouped into units (words) which the successful reader sounds out in his mind's ear as he goes along, conjuring up a visual image in his mind's eye of what they are supposed to depict. He is able to follow the flow of meaning as the words are grouped into phrases and clauses to form total expressions of thoughts in complete sentences. By recalling how words sound, and the necessary physical efforts required to reproduce these sounds, he can, when the occasion requires, verbalize the words by reading aloud. As he proceeds along a printed page, if he encounters a new or unfamiliar word, he is able to break it down into its component parts, and compare these parts with sounds that he already knows. By blending his visual and auditory skills, he successfully masters reading. To most of us adults all of these functions are so automatic that we find it impossible to recall how we learned to read and just what skills are involved in this intricate process.

And intricate it is, as any attempt to study all the processes involved will demonstrate. Figure 5 shows the mechanisms involved in the acts of communicating: reception of the sensory stimulus, processing of the information it contains, and then expression through one of the three methods of symbolization. The stimulus may be visual alone, as in reading from a printed page, auditory alone, as in listening to the radio, or a combination of the two, as in listening to a visible speaker and watching his actions while he talks. In some instances the stimulus may involve the sensations of position and touch, as in Braille-reading by the blind. Once the sensory stimulation occurs and the flow of nervous impulses from the eye or ear starts, the brain begins the act of perception. It compares and contrasts one particular stimulus to others, by interpreting its significance and determining whether it will require a response, and by placing it into its proper position in reference to other stimuli being received. How well this perceptive function is performed is directly affected by the ability of the individual to direct his attention to the stimulus and block out conflicting stimuli. This in turn is influenced by the emotional state of the individual which may interfere both with his ability to concentrate on the stimulus and his ability to perform the next step in the communication process which we call cognitive functioning. Here the individual utilizes his previous experiences to help evaluate the type of response he should make, trying to recall them from his short-term memory or else taking time to dig into his long-term memory stores, usually making associations with similar stimuli. This capability is a reflection of and is dependent upon the intellectual state of the individual, and it permits him to carry out the expressive act appropriate to the situation. The individual selects the proper symbol to convey his idea, and by speaking, writing or gesturing, or a combination of these, completes his act of communication. His ability to perform all these functions correctly is closely related to his spatial and temporal orientation. Once he successfully communicates, the continuation of his efforts is contingent upon the response of those with whom he is attempting to communicate.

Learning to read actually begins long before the child enters the first grade, for every step along the road to developmental maturity that we discussed in our first chapter adds to the foundation necessary for the child to attain what one reporter has called "the last skill acquired." The newborn baby first becomes aware of the world about him through gross sensations such as relative warmth and bodily position. He soon experiences discomfort in the form of hunger, which he finds can be relieved

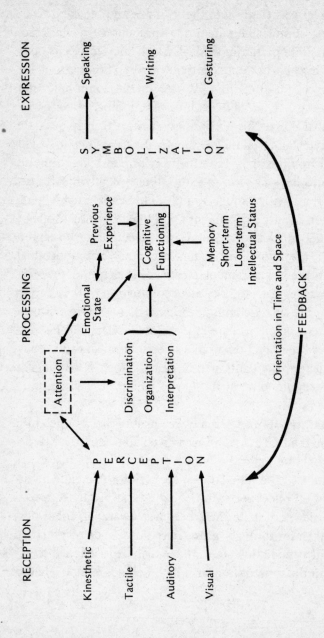

Figure 5. Diagrammatic Representation of the Communicative Skills

The four sensory modalities required to begin the act of communicating are kinesthetic (position-sense), tactile (touch), auditory (hearing) and visual (seeing). They receive the sensations which are then passed up to the nervous system for perception. At this point the individual discriminates and interprets these sensations, comparing them with other sensations and organizing them for transmittal to the higher centers where cognitive functioning occurs. Depending upon previous experience and the ability to recall impressions through short- and long-term memory, and that vaguely understood capability that we call intellectual status, the individual is now prepared to respond appropriately to the stimulus. His response utilizes the symbols which allow him to express his ideas by speaking, writing or moving his hands, face and body in the proper gestures.

The entire act of communication is dependent upon the ability of the individual to pay attention to the source and character of the stimulus, shutting out other distracting stimuli which might interfere with his ability to process the information, and respond with the appropriate expression. This ability is strongly influenced by his emotional state, since tension or anxiety can serve as a potent interfering force to both perception and cognitive activity. Confused orientation in time and space can help keep the individual so disorganized that he is unable to develop the essential processing skills needed in communication. The character of communication is influenced by a special type of feedback derived from an internal monitoring system whereby an individual hears himself speak or watches and feels himself write. His continuing performance is influenced by his own evaluation of what he is doing and is altered accordingly. This differs from the external type of feedback noted in Figures 2 and 3 which is a social reinforcement depending upon the type of response received from those with whom the developing child deals.

in a certain manner which is related to smell and taste. He can see and is soon actually able to make some visual discrimination between forms and colors. He is capable of hearing noises and will respond to the loud ones and other objectionable stimuli with movements of his entire body. As he matures he recognizes his mother and others who tend to him and, if all goes well, follows the road to developmental maturity previously described. Every day each new experience readies him for the time he will be expected to sit still in the classroom and follow the teacher's instructions as she guides him to the understanding that the little symbols and figures on the printed page are supposed to represent something, and that this something is associated with a particular sound or group of sounds. If when he was younger he had a dog, he learned that this animal made a sound like bow-wow, and he may have actually used this sound as the symbolic representation for the animal ("See the bow-wow? Nice bow-wow. Pet the bow-wow"). As he grew older he found that most people referred to the bow-wow as dog, and if he had any picture books he could associate the graphic representation with both the sound as he uttered it and the animal it was supposed to represent.

Now in the classroom he meets an old friend and finds that if he can repeat this word — and others — to his teacher's satisfaction he is rewarded, and every few weeks he can take home a note of approval for his proud parents to sign. As he makes further progress he is able to build upon his previous knowledge and experience to add new words to his vocabulary. By blending what he hears with what he has heard and seen before, he soon learns to master new words, and then put them together into units in their proper syntax. Next he finds that with the proper skill he can learn to express himself in writing, first by printing the same letters he sees in a book and later by using cursive writing, which is a much easier method, since all the letters in a word are connected. If he has developed proper spatial concepts he can distribute the words evenly along the page, and if he has no lack of skill with his fingers, hands and arms and no defect in body-part awareness, he can make the pencil go along the page at his command without any real difficulty. He learns that all words aren't written or spelled exactly as they sound, so he must call on his visual memory to aid his auditory recall — plus a few memorized rules, like i before e except after c. Sooner or later he masters the basic purpose of reading which is to be able to absorb ideas from what is printed on the page of his textbook and later to put those ideas down on paper when the teacher instructs him to do so.

But what of our child with MBD? To begin with he may never have been around a dog as a little boy, especially if his level of emotional immaturity kept him frightened of all strange things. But even if he went through the same experiences as his non-disabled friends, the results were quite different. His interpretation of early sensory experiences was distorted and lacked proper self-identification and orientation in space, and he did not enjoy many relationships with people. Thus his feedback and subsequent progress were altered. His immature perception and interpretation of the things he sees and hears persist beyond the usual age and when he attempts to reproduce them he may be met with laughter and scorn from his classmates. For some reason he cannot blend his auditory and visual reception satisfactorily and one may predominate. If he is strong in hearing but is weak visually, he will spell words as they sound; brother becomes "bruther," ocean is "oshun." If he is strong visually, and weak auditorily, he will lack the skill to break down new words phonetically, and will have to rely upon his vision to memorize the whole word together. He may be able to remember a long word like "superficial" because it has many clues, but the short words such as "the" and "on" offer much confusion.

Added to this basic difficulty in mastering the skills involved in language, the child with MBD has all the other problems we mentioned earlier — short attention span, distractibility, right-left confusion, and fine motor incordination so that he just cannot make the pencil do what he wants it to. Since he also has all the elements of emotional immaturity to contend with, he becomes easily frustrated when things don't go right. If, while writing, he is frequently erasing line after line, he may finally tear up the whole page in a livid rage. (The type of feedback that he receives from his teacher for this behavior is *not* likely to encourage the development of any feeling of self-esteem.) The more he struggles with his problem, the more he seems to be misunderstood. His teacher often keeps insisting he could do better if he tried harder and encourages his parents to put more pressure on him. As failure follows failure his opinion of himself sinks lower and lower — and as if that wasn't enough every six weeks he has to carry home documented evidence of how poorly he is doing.

How can we use our knowledge of the problem to help the LD child overcome his difficulties? Suppose the teacher stands in front of the class and says, "All right, children, get out your paper and pencil, we're going to have a quiz. Be sure to write your name in the upper right hand corner, and put the date below your name. Now, the first question is: Who wrote the Declaration of Independence?" To begin with, our LD child has to be paying attention. If someone were whispering to him, or if someone had scraped a chair, he may not have heard her at all, or perhaps not everything she said. And even though he may have heard, if he has a sequential memory deficiency, he is going to have to struggle to follow her directions in the proper order — *all that*, before he can begin to cope with the actual answer. Next, he must be able to interpret properly what the teacher asked, then start sliding open the filing cabinets in his mind until he finds the folder that says "American Revolution," riff through George Washington, John Adams, John Hancock, Thomas Jefferson, Benjamin Franklin and the others until he decides upon the correct one. Next he has to see in his mind's eye exactly what the words "Thomas Jefferson" look like and make his hand go across the paper to reproduce that visual image graphically. He doesn't have all day, for the teacher is standing there waiting to ask the next question!

So in an instant — almost automatically — the child has to call on auditory and visual perception, and recall and utilize kinesthetic and tactile methods to aid his performance. For most children — those without MBD — this usually offers no difficulty. They can perform these automatic tasks without a great deal of effort. I have explained to parents and teachers that we can better understand this if we remember how we drive an automobile. When you first learned this skill (if you began on the old stick-shift as I did) you will remember how you even had to look at the key to see which way it went in the ignition. Then you jerked a few times with the clutch, maybe killing the motor in the process. But with a bit more experience and practice you were able to master this accomplishment. Now you can rush into the car, reach into your purse without looking to pull out the keys, put them into the ignition switch and start the car without interrupting your conversation. Then you can drive from home to town avoiding collisions with other automobiles by making hundreds of intricate decisions about their speed and direction, stop for the proper signals, continually glancing at the rear-view mirror and then ahead to keep track of the flow of traffic, not run over small children and errant animals, turn the proper corners and reach your destination safely. You may even plan your dinner menu and make out a shopping list in your mind, and all the while drive along without mishap. If someone met you as you got out of your car and asked you to tell them everything you said and heard on the way to town — you couldn't do it! When you start the car you turn on an automatic pilot and, although completely alert and in command of your senses, you don't really do a lot of deep thinking about driving. Most children in school do the same about classroom routine, so that they are able to apply their thinking mechanisms to those functions that really require them. They shut out distractions automatically, much as we do when driving, and are able to attend to the matters at hand properly. The child with MBD is incapable of doing this and soon finds himself out of the mainstream of classroom activity. If, in addition, he is emotionally upset, is anticipating failure even before he tries, and if this is one of his bad days, the results of his performance are a foregone conclusion. This lack of ability to perform automatically, shutting out distractions and concentrating correctly, is one of the least appreciated difficulties facing the child with MBD. It is almost as if he were trying to drive his car but had to stop at each corner to look at the street signs in order to get reorganized, then start up again, only to pause and try to look at every storefront window along the way, falling continually further behind the traffic and watching everyone else pass him by.

Reading involves much more than being able to recognize different designs and geometric forms and to distinguish certain sounds and reproduce them. The good reader must also be able to follow the flow of ideas being expressed, raising his voice with the proper inflections when emphasis is required, softening his volume when indicated, placing the accent on the correct syllable and maintaining a smooth verbal continuum that almost anticipates the next phrase as he moves along. If you have ever listened to one of the more inept newscasters on a small radio station as he drearily plods along, chopping the phrases with a monotonous uni-syllable effect: "Today-we-have-an-oth-er-re-port-from-Wash-ing-ton-sta-ting-that-Pres-i-dent-Nix-on-will-give-an-oth-er-tel-e-vi-sion-re-port-to-the-coun-try-a-bout-his-bud-get," perhaps stumbling over one or two of the phrases, repeating some, with some vocal pauses, such as "uh-uh," scattered through the entire garbled mess, you will recall how difficult it is to follow the *meaning* of what is being read. The learning-disabled child who stands in front of his classmates and gives such a labored presentation is sure to be greeted by laughter and ridicule both during and after his efforts, if he has courage enough to complete them. The disorganization, distractibility and conceptual difficulties that make up such a major portion of the MBD complex come to the fore on such occasions.

What is particularly frustrating to the LD child is the fact that he can usually express himself verbally with much more ease if he is speaking his own mind rather than vocalizing the printed word. Just as the stutterer who finds that his disability does not show itself when he is singing a familiar song, the dyslexic child can *talk* (with reasonably good skill and aptitude) as long as he knows what is coming next and can group his own ideas. His disorganization may occasionally confuse him and his anomia may cause him to grope for a proper word now and then — don't we all have this problem? But the difference between his ability to communicate by speaking and his reading skill — or lack of it — is striking.

There can be no doubt that many children can be aided by any one of a number of techniques now available for remedial education, provided the difficulty is detected early enough to avoid the severe emotional effects caused by school failure. By removing the child from a pressure-laden situation and devoting individual, or one-to-one, attention to his problems, much can be accomplished. But there are so many children involved and so few teachers with the time, interest and knowledge to work in a lengthy remedial program, that many children will have to be abandoned if we continue in our present state.

One of the greatest difficulties the MBD child brings with him into the classroom is his short attention span. Research now indicates that this disorder is associated with a chemical deficiency, and that it can be greatly counteracted by medication. The ability to organize material as it is perceived, to concentrate attention and shut out distractions is a function of areas in the brain stem which are collectively called the reticular formation. These areas have many connections with the portion of the brain known as the limbic system, which has important functions in behavior and emotions. They also have a number of connections with the cerebral cortex, the true thinking area of the brain (see Figures 6 and 7). The efficiency of transmission of nerve impulses in the brain stem is related to a group of substances called nor-adrenalin, one of which is a sort of chemical first-cousin to adrenalin. Certain medications such as the amphetamines, methylphenidate, imipramine and nortriptylene have been found to affect the amount of nor-adrenalin in the brain stem, either by increasing its formation or by preventing its breakdown and subsequent re-absorption into the blood stream (Figure 8). By enhancing the function of the regulating mechanisms in the sub-brain and

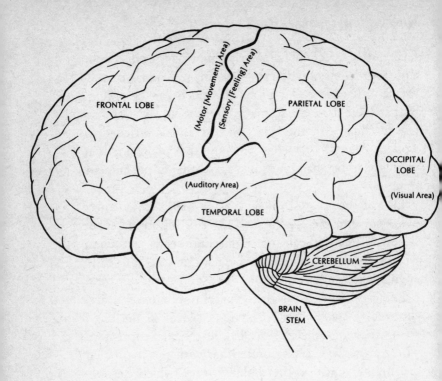

Figure 6. Outer Surface of Brain

The outer surface of the brain as seen from the left side, showing the divisions of areas into lobes. The outermost layer of brain cells is called the cerebral cortex. The localization of various functions in the adult brain is shown.

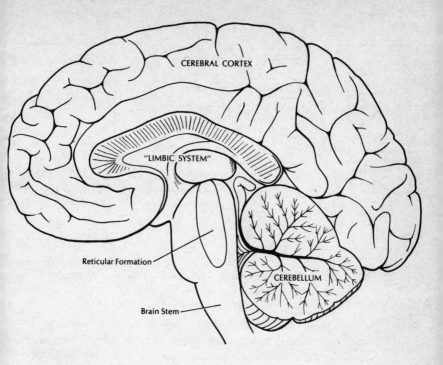

Figure 7. Cross Section of Center of Brain

The middle surface of the brain as seen if split down the center, showing the relationship of the reticular formation in the brain stem, thought to be concerned in the coordination of automatic functions, and the limbic system, thought to be important in the control of emotional responses.

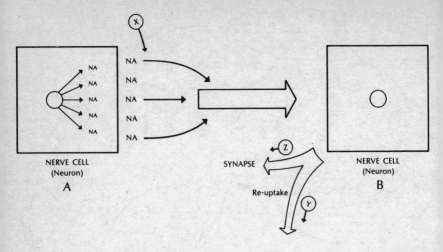

Figure 8. Diagrammatic Picture of the Transmission of an Impulse in the Reticular Formation of the Brain

The transmission of an impulse from one nerve cell (neuron) to the next across the space between the two cells (called the synapse) is influenced by certain chemicals among which is nor-adrenalin. This diagram shows how nor-adrenalin is produced within the nerve cell and released (X) to help carry the impulse over to the next neuron, after which the chemical is inactivated by re-uptake either into the general circulation (Y) or back to neuron A (Z). Certain medications such as the amphetamines, methylphenidate, imipramine, and nortriptylene seem to improve the functions of the brain stem by increasing the formation of nor-adrenalin or by preventing its re-uptake, thus making more of the chemical available at the site of nerve impulse transmission. These medications are ordinarily classified as stimulants but in MBD they appear to selectively stimulate the function of the cells in the reticular formation, thus improving the ability of the child to shut out distractions, lengthen his attention span, and reduce his disorganization through curtailment of the amount of random stimulation reaching the cortex.

brain stem, these medications, ordinarily considered as stimulants, produce what was first thought of as a paradoxical effect. The child actually appeared to be more relaxed and at ease, as the medication reduced the excessive flow of uncontrolled stimuli to the upper brain. With improved organization and a marked reduction of distractibility he found himself better able to cope with the normal classroom routine and became much more responsive to whatever remedial techniques were made available to him.

The study of methods to help the child with learning disability has demonstrated that the use of a multi-sensory approach can often bring about a great improvement in the child's academic performance. By having him trade letters and words as he says them and looks at them, even by having him feel his throat as he says them, the instructor makes him employ kinesthetic and tactile sensations to reinforce the visual and auditory ones. By having him trace in sand or clay, additional reinforcement is given. Letters that are made of wood or plastic can be handled and studied by the child individually or in a group to give a three-dimensional approach. Simply allowing the child to read aloud and follow the words with his finger may be of some value. Other multi-sensory approaches involve the use of color-coded words and phrases and special templates for tracing, while some remedial techniques use visual and auditory perceptual training to help the child recognize basic shapes and sounds.

In spite of the encouraging advances made by the recognition of the problem in the early grades, and through improved remedial techniques and more widely applied chemotherapy, there remains a group of children who continue to have great difficulty with reading. When attempting to explain this phenomenon to parents, I have found that they grasp the problem more readily if we liken reading skills and talents to musical skills and talents. Some people are born with the ability to sing beautifully without taking a lesson, while others couldn't carry a tune if it were wrapped up with a handle on it! Could it be possible that there are some children born tone-deaf for reading — hard-core dyslexics who can never become fluent readers just as some individuals can never be taught to be good singers? If there are such individuals, they should be identified and treated differently, since reading is but one means for the acquisition of knowledge. For them other ways to learning should be stressed: they should be allowed to take tape recorders to school and be given their examinations orally. This might be difficult to accomplish in a school system with a rigid classroom routine and an inflexible curriculum, but with the school of the future turning to open classrooms and more individualized instruction, we have hope that the day is not too distant when every single school child will be given the opportunity to achieve his true educational potential.

One of the most promising of all the recent studies on reading disorders — one that should be of tremendous value in specifically helping us understand why Steve can't read and, most important of all, what we can do to help him and others like him — is the report by Elena Boder on children with reading disorders in the Los Angeles school system. Going back to the pioneering work of Helmer Myklebust, who described auditory dyslexia and visual dyslexia, Dr. Boder has developed an evaluation process by which she is able to classify all dyslexic children into three groups: the first composed of those who are strong in visual capabilities, but weak auditorily; the second in which the reverse is true — auditory strength and low visual weakness are common; and the third, in which the children have weaknesses in both areas. Since the tendency among remedial experts now is to work through the child's own individual strengths rather than to attempt to correct his weaknesses, the therapeutic implications are readily obvious. The child in the first group, who is able to visualize words but lacks auditory skill, needs a program based on whole-word techniques, rather than phonics, which is his weakness. The child in the second group would profit most from a phonetic approach. The child in the third group, who may be the hard-core dyslexic we mentioned before, will require a multi-sensory program with amplification of both methods. We will discuss Dr. Boder's screening program and her therapeutic suggestions more fully in Chapter 10.

One final point needs to be stressed again. Steve's reading difficulty is only one phase of the problem and, if we are to truly appreciate why he has been unable to master this important skill, we have to go back over his entire educational and developmental history. Dyslexia is not the only symptom that Steve has shown. He has also demonstrated the disorders of activity, behavior and thought which are the bases for his disability, and he has shown the short attention span, distractibility, and behavioral immaturity so characteristic of MBD. If we are to give him the comprehensive assistance he so desperately needs, we will have to bring together the learning-disability team of teacher, parent and physician and combine their efforts in the right direction, aiming at the same goal.

PART TWO

INTRODUCTION:
THE BLIND MEN AND THE ELEPHANT

The problems of the learning-disabled child, especially reading disorders, have been described in professional writings for over three quarters of a century. They were first reported almost simultaneously in the 1890s by three separate English physicians, one a doctor for a boys' school, the second a public health officer, the third an ophthalmologist. All three commented on the fact that their patients were mostly boys, that they had normal intelligence, and that they had unexplainable difficulties in trying to learn to read. In the many years that have followed their pioneering studies, these observations have appeared over and over again: a preponderance of males is involved, and they have normal intellectual abilities but baffling problems with communication skills. When attempts to interpret these disorders on the same basis as those of adults with reading difficulties failed, investigators began to search for other causes to explain what they called "congenital word-blindness." By this time a tremendous surge of interest in the behavioral sciences had developed. These sciences offered an explanation for all educational disorders on the grounds of emotional maladjustment. This concept became so firmly entrenched that it still strongly influences teacher training and theories about child management. But it has failed to be of any appreciable use in the improvement of reading disorders. During the 1930s and 1940s, two giants appeared on the learning disability scene: Samuel Orton, the neuropsychiatrist from Iowa whose studies on children's reading and writing problems opened the door to a rational approach to these difficulties, and Alfred Strauss, who first described in detail the behavioral characteristics that we have come to associate with the MBD child. A number of their observations were of necessity speculative, since they lacked the knowledge of neurology and biochemistry available to us now, but their contributions have profoundly influenced our thinking.

It has been almost impossible for interested workers to keep abreast of the advances in every field concerned with learning disabilities. Psychologists rarely have an opportunity to read medical journals, physicians seldom see the psychological literature, and classroom teachers don't have a chance to see either. Accordingly, a number of misconceptions have developed concerning the causes of learning disorders and the remediation techniques available, and many parents have followed the same heartbreaking, frustrating routine that Steve's mother described to me. Each method is advocated with enthusiasm and almost a religious fervor, and the personality of the advocate has a strong influence on the parents. The conscientious adviser who wants to guide parents in finding help for their learning-disabled child, while at the same time protecting them from those who would exploit the situation for their own financial gain, will find it difficult to evaluate the enthusiastic claims made for some of the methods of treatment currently in vogue. The zeal of the advocates of one particular method may sufficiently obscure any attempt to obtain a truly objective viewpoint. The counselor finds it difficult to decide who is sincere but misguided, who is taking advantage of current confusion for their own purposes, and who can truly give some much-needed assistance to the child and his concerned parents. The American Medical Association has published a booklet to help physicians reach an equitable decision concerning new and controversial claims in medical fields, pointing out that patients should be advised to avoid those who publish laudatory articles in popular lay periodicals without submitting their claims to proper scientific investigation, who claim persecution by the medical profession because of fear of competition, or who proclaim that their method of treatment is the only proper one or is far superior to any other technique. Responsible scientific organizations have accepted their duty and called attention to those claimants who have followed these misleading tactics.

Because first impressions are so lasting, and since it is more difficult to unlearn something than to make a fresh beginning, many misconceptions concerning learning disabilities have been advanced and accepted, and not discarded even though newer knowledge became available. As each worker became more deeply involved in his own discipline he tended to ignore or was unaware of the advances taking place in other areas. The divisions that separate the educational, psychological and medical professions have further served to widen the gaps that prevent comprehensive understanding of the learning-disabled child.

The present confusion calls to mind the classic fable

of the blind men and the elephant. You remember the story — how each touched a different part of the animal and thought he knew what it was on the basis of his own limited impression. The one holding the trunk said it must be a snake; the one feeling the tusk insisted it was a spear; the one touching the ear said it was a fan; the one with his arms around a leg stated it was a tree; the one pulling on the tail said it must be a rope, while the last one, pushing against the animal's side, proclaimed that the others were all wrong, for it must be a wall! The LD child has been the victim of the same kind of short-sighted approach by well-intentioned professionals, each of whom has just enough knowledge of his own field but each of whom refuses to step back and try to picture the whole problem. Let's examine these attitudes and see how these false prophets have added to the confusion surrounding LD children and how their prejudices have held many parents back from seeking competent advice to help their child.

4.

"LEAVE HIM ALONE, HE'LL OUTGROW IT"

The first of the blind men who has led us astray by his combination of false logic and gross misinformation carries a banner with a most appealing slogan that says, "Leave him alone, he'll outgrow it." He has attracted quite a large following for there is just enough sense in what he preaches to sound reasonable. Who can find fault with the following kind of argument? Since so many of the findings we describe in the learning-disabled child are simply those of immaturity, why not just give him a little more time to see if he won't mature on his own? Aren't most parents unduly overanxious about their own children, comparing their developmental progress with all their little cousins and the other children in the neighborhood? Since the doctors agree that the problems of the LD child are due to a developmental lag rather than a true disease of the nervous system, why not wait for this lag to disappear, which it might do if given the chance to? Besides, since there is no absolutely certain diagnostic test to prove what is wrong with the child, wouldn't it be safer not to meddle with him and wait to see if he won't outgrow all his trouble?

Many of the parents of my LD patients tell me the sad story of how they waited and waited, until they discovered that the only thing their child outgrew was his trousers! Year after year they expected their "late bloomer" to blossom forth and catch up with the rest of the class, but instead he became more frustrated and humiliated by the ridicule he received from his classmates and his teachers. Who can blame a child when he begins to hate school and all it stands for, if he has to go forth every day and compete with his classmates who seem to be able to do with ease all the things which are so difficult for him? If he is overactive and creates a disturbance in the classroom, he soon is labelled by his teacher as a troublemaker — and don't think that one teacher doesn't pass along this information to her next year's successor: "Oh, you're going to have Stevie next year. Well, let me tell you about him!" When the child finds that he has established a reputation which precedes him into his new classroom, he often accepts it without question and does his best to live up to it, thus perpetuating the impending catastrophe. The new teacher knew all along what he was like, and he doesn't disappoint her.

By the time the learning-disabled child reaches junior high school, the damage to his personality has become so intense that he is almost beyond salvaging. His opinion of himself is so low, and his lack of self-confidence has become so deeply imbedded, that remedial instruction must take a back seat to efforts at restoring his self-esteem. Since nothing succeeds like success, attempts must be made to find out what can be done to give the child some experience of having made accomplishments in those areas in which he is proficient, and thereby break up the vicious circle in which he has been trapped. Otherwise he may easily continue his inexorable march through suspension after suspension to eventual expulsion from school, and the correlation between dropping out of school and delinquency has been too well established to need further elaboration here. Our correctional institutions are filled to overflowing with young people who were allowed to go along without special help to see if they wouldn't outgrow their difficulties.

Once this pattern is recognized, it must follow that all concerned with handling the developing child — the teacher, parents, physician, counselor, and people from other disciplines — will want to intervene at the proper time and in the proper manner to prevent this unfortunate sequence from taking place. Because every child is just a bit different, and because the characteristics of the MBD child are so subtle and variable, there are no clear-cut findings to help us in this endeavor. If we review the figures in the first section of this book and look over the activity and behavior mannerisms listed, we will discover that some of them can be found in nearly every child at one time or another. How can we be sure that we are not just being overconcerned about usual childhood variations, and where do we draw the line between what is normal and abnormal? Since inquisitive activity is such a standard feature of developing children what should be classified as *hyper*activity? What distinguishes a child who throws a tantrum in order to have his way, if he has found this method effective in the past, from a child whose lack of control has a biochemical basis? And how do you tell an MBD child with an attention-span deficit from a child who is just stubborn and refuses to mind his parents?

Alas, there is no magic formula to guide us, so our false prophet has no difficulty in picking up a sizeable group of

advocates. "Why, he's just all boy — you don't understand boys," his mother will be told by a well-meaning
grandmother, or: "Spare the rod and spoil the child,"
advises an annoyed neighbor. The confused mother who
senses that her son is truly *different* from most of his
friends, or the bewildered father who has already found
that physical punishment is *not* the answer, soon become
defensive at this unwarranted criticism of their offspring.
And when his teacher suggests that his behavior and poor
performance in the classroom are the direct result of poor
preparation and training at home, and recommends that
his parents take away some of his privileges until he learns
how to pay attention better and apply himself in school
— a disciplinary procedure they have already been trying
to no avail — their frustration climbs to the breaking
point. They look back in wonderment in an effort to discover where they have failed their child. As concerned
parents they have read about the importance of socio-
cultural deprivation as a cause of poor school performance, that early stimulation to give the developing child
many diverse sight and sound experiences is so vital for
training in reading skills, and that a warm, loving home
atmosphere will give a child the security necessary to adjust to the new situations he will encounter in the classrooms. So they devote time to give him their undivided
attention, buy educational toys for him, see that he
watches "Sesame Street" and all the other good television
programs, take him to the zoo and museums — and he
still cannot keep up with his classmates when he enters
school. They try to adopt as calm and objective an attitude as possible (insofar as any parents can be totally ob-

jective about their own child) and listen to those who suggest the natural way is best, that a little more patience and time will take care of everything.

Unfortunately, while they are waiting, time moves along its own stubborn course, school day following school day and semester following semester. At times predetermined by the particular local school situations, tests are given which are supposed to reveal how much each child has learned from what the teacher has been presenting, and the results of these examinations are duly marked down as a record of the child's progress. Then at intervals also dictated by local protocol, each child is given to take home for all to see a written document upon which his successes or failures are irrevocably inscribed. When the results of these periodical pronouncements are less than satisfactory, the teacher and parents shortly arrange a conference in the hope of arriving at a satisfactory solution to the problem. If no one really understands the underlying basis for the MBD child's poor performance, the usual corrective measures do not help the situation, and the child reaches the end of the school year without attaining the level necessary for promotion to the next grade.

Since the obvious answer to the problem would appear to be holding the child back until he is ready to advance, the teacher, if she is a "leave-him-aloner," will recommend that the child be retained and allowed to repeat the grade. This requires the child to see and hear again all the same things that he encountered previously, which he soon finds very boring. However this time he is surrounded by a new group of classmates, most of whom are younger than he is and many of whom have developed a bond from having all been together the previous year. Sensing that something is a bit different about our MBD child, they soon begin to treat him as an outsider, poking fun at his differences and laughing at his inadequacies. If the learning-disabled child is able to survive this emotional strain and does happen to catch on to enough of the material in the classroom to justify promotion, he may be advanced the next time, so that the scarring from the previous experiences may not be repeated. Usually, however, his learning disability persists, and after another year or so a new teacher confers with his parents to decide whether or not to hold him back again. I have seen children who have repeated the first grade twice, the third or fourth grade again, and now at the sixth-grade level are being considered for repetition once more!

Irrespective of the academic aspects, the devastating effects of this developmental mismanagement in crushing the child's morale and lowering his self-esteem should be obvious. When a child is an underachiever in the classroom something is wrong, and if his poor academic performance is accompanied by attention-span and memory deficits, by perceptual-concept deficiencies, and by the peculiar patterns of ineptness in the language skills we have previously described, the possibility of specific learning disability should be the *first* condition that comes to mind. At the pre-school level, if a child has hyperactivity or clumsiness or emotional instability which is truly excessive compared to most children his age, or that persists beyond the usual time limits expected for improvement, minimal brain dysfunction should be seriously considered as a likely basis for his troubles, and attempts should be made to help him before his learning difficulties are added to his burdens. "Watch and wait" may be an excellent credo for many childhood problems, but the importance of school experiences to the development of the child's self-image and personality indicate that non-intervention may be a total disaster. Recognition of the deficiencies of our current fixed educational system and the restrictions placed on all children who must be subjected to them has produced a tremendous amount of interest and enthusiasm for corrective changes in the classroom and in teacher attitudes. But educators must realize that a sizeable proportion of the classroom population is different in chemical makeup from the rest of the class and that these children need to be handled properly if they are to derive full benefit from any innovations in their educational experiences. The fact that these children do not *look* different from their classmates, that their behavioral and performance difficulties might be caused by non-environmental factors, does not relieve us from the responsibility of recognizing the true nature of their disorder and the means of therapy presently available for them.

One last note about developmental progress and the natural ability of children to overcome some of the problems of learning disabilities is in order. If MBD is in most instances an inherited disorder, as it seems to be, then obviously there are many adults who have had this condition — or still do — and have been able to adjust successfully and become responsible citizens who can make meaningful contributions to their communities. I must admit that in talking to parents of children with learning disabilities, I learned that some of them were indeed able to get along without help and have survived their ordeal. Some have told me that along about the fifth or sixth grade "everything seemed to fall into place," and from then on they did well. Others tell me that even as adults they don't really enjoy reading, or that they still have trouble with spelling, or that they still can't understand math. However, none of them want their children to go through what they did unaided or to take the chance that their children will eventually outgrow their problems. They know their child will be six years old — or seven, or eight — only once in his lifetime and, if there is any chance to help him do better at that age level, they are anxious to do anything possible. The loudest advocates of the "leave-them-alone" school are those who have no children of their own with learning disabilities, or who have never been around them at home or in the classroom. When they point out that Woodrow Wilson did not learn to read until he was nine or ten, that General Patton had to be tutored to get into West Point, and that Hans Christian Andersen showed the characteristic spelling and handwriting distortions of learning disability in the original scripts of his stories, all we can do is nod in agreement, but point out that in our present state of knowledge — or ignorance — we have no way to predict which road any individual child will take. We do know that some do not turn out so fortunately, as is indicated, for example, in this letter from a physician concerning

one individual with learning disability who did not outgrow his problem.

The material . . . furnished me, in my judgment amply
documents the impression that _____ had a specific language disability . . . which (unfortunately as is true of a
great many persons) was not recognized by his various teachers nor by the several psychological examinations he was
given.

I think that this disability and its consequential effect
upon him . . . is relevant since it amplifies the impression
from many sources about the nature of _____'s estrange-
ment from people, his diffident truculence during school
years and his unwarranted estimation of his literary capacities. . . .

For a bright young person to be handicapped in the use of
language is an especially galling experience. It seems to me
that in _____'s instance this frustration gave an added
impetus to his need to prove to the world that he was an
unrecognized "great man" . . . .

Reading disability, as part of a specific language disability,
is a defect akin to color blindness or tone deafness and is
not a sign of stupidity, or wilful inattention or necessarily
indicative of a lack of education — although it is frequently
taken to be equated with those devalued social be-
haviors. . . .

The high social value placed upon adequate literate performance by our culture invokes sanctions of considerable
significance. . . . Inasmuch as they tend to lose status in
the eyes of their peers as well as superiors (teachers, parents,
and adults), they are prone to develop a range of alternative
ways of coping with their disadvantaged state: apparent in-
difference, truculent resistance, and other displacement activities by which they hope to cover up their deficiency and
appear in a more commendable light. . . . Frequently there

is a misattribution of responsibility to various real and fancied psychological and social circumstances which are then made to appear as casual.

In contrast to a first-hand examination which is indispensable for a psychiatric evaluation, one can establish a diagnosis of a specific language disability from written productions. Consequently, I feel I can say with a greater degree of confidence that the written material attributed to _____ that I have had the opportunity to review is consistent with the clinical picture one sees in individuals with this disability.

This remarkably clear report of learning disability and its effects on the personality was written by Dr. Howard P. Rome, a senior psychiatric consultant at the Mayo Clinic. It was his response to a request by the Warren Commission for a study — the subject, Lee Harvey Oswald.

5.

"HE MUST BE MENTALLY RETARDED"

The second false prophet waves a banner with a slogan which suggests that the real reason our learning-disabled child cannot learn is that he lacks the intellectual equipment necessary to make proper classroom progress. His argument has an appeal to many educators, and physicians as well, who like to divide children into broad categories, and for whom these divisions have to be rigid and clear cut. Since at one time school children were supposedly capable of learning at the same rate, those who did not were all considered to be mentally deficient or retarded. Soon after he began school, or sometimes even before, each child was pigeon-holed and assigned either to a regular classroom or to a special class where teaching methods could be adapted to allow him to learn at a slower rate by presenting the materials over and over again in a simplified form, in the hope that the child would eventually better absorb the material taught in this manner. Educators recognized that there were varying degrees of severity in mental retardation, so these children were further subdivided and labelled as "educable mentally retarded" (EMR) or "trainable mentally retarded" (TMR) depending upon the scores obtained on tests given them. This new terminology replaced "moron" and "imbecile." ("Idiot" was applied to those so severely retarded that they were neither educable nor trainable.) Parents of these unfortunate children banded together to spur interest in the problems of their retarded children and were able to influence legislatures into appropriating considerable sums of money that permitted educators to establish special programs in the regular school systems. The programs allowed many of these children to be kept at home rather than consigned to institutional care.

In order to determine which children should be assigned to these special classes, tests were devised to measure intelligence and express the results in numbers, so that each child could be placed on a scale and compared to others. The first such test was developed by a psychologist, Alfred Binet, who worked on this problem with a physician named Theophile Simon in the early 1900s on an assignment from the French government. After abandoning a number of methods that varied from comparison of head sizes and handwriting to palmistry, they tried out groups of problems of different complexity on children of varying ages to see if they could thus tell at what age an appropriate feat of intelligence could usually be accomplished. The Binet-Simon scales thus developed were applied to see if a given child could solve those tests that most children of the same age could, and, from the number that he did correctly above, below, and at his own age level, his "mental age" was calculated. These tests were later standardized for use in this country by an American, Lewis M. Terman, working at Stanford University, hence the name Stanford-Binet. The term "IQ," meaning intelligence quotient, is obtained when the mental age is divided by the chronological (calendar) age and that figure multiplied by 100. The child of ten years who only scores a mental age of six is said to have an IQ of 60; if his mental age is twelve, his IQ is 120. The normal range is considered to vary from 80 to 120, with the educable retarded usually considered in the 50–80 range and the trainable from 30 to 50.

Many other tests have been developed since then, the most popular of which was devised by David Wechsler at Bellevue Hospital in New York. It is called the Wechsler Intelligence Scale for Children, which is abbreviated WISC (and affectionately called by psychologists the "whisk," just like the broom). This test has the advantage of subdividing the child's abilities and inabilities so that a competent observer can report to the teacher or remedial educator exactly where the individual child needs help. Since most of my experience has been in working with examiners who favor the WISC, let us look at the different portions of the test and see exactly what it involves.

The WISC is divided into two sections, the verbal tests, which measure essentially what the child has learned and understands from what he hears, and the performance tests, which determine how well the child learns from what he sees. Each section is comprised of six separate subtests which are designed to cover as wide a group of activities as possible. The examples given are not the actual questions used in the test, but are similar enough to allow the reader to understand the basic principles involved.

VERBAL SUBTESTS

1. *Information*

The child is questioned about his knowledge of general information, such as "Who was the first man to land on the moon?" "What is the capital of France?" "How many nickels make a dime?" This is intended to test the child's alertness to the world about him and how well he remembers from his experiences.

2. *Comprehension*

Measures practical sense and understanding. The child is asked, "What is the advantage of keeping money in a bank?" "What would you do if you saw the house next door on fire?" This tests the child's ability to draw on his knowledge and experience to handle real life situations, and to some degree his ability to hold back impulsive behavior.

3. *Arithmetic*

The child is given mathematical problems of increasing difficulty, which he must compute in his head and respond to orally; a few of the problems are printed for the child to read. ("If two apples cost fifteen cents, how much will a dozen cost?") This tests attention, concentration and reasoning; the child must have good auditory memory and visualization and be able to follow an oral sequence.

4. Similarities

The child is asked "In what way is an apple like an orange?" "How are paper and coal alike?" "We walk with our feet, we throw with our ————." This tells how well the child can use information to reach a logical conclusion, how much he understands about relationships, categories, and abstract ideas.

5. Vocabulary

The child must define words such as table, glove, bicycle, microscope, nuisance. This measures auditory memory and comprehension as well as the ability to verbalize ideas. The examiner observes not only the correctness of the answer, but the quality of the child's expression.

6. Digit Span

Numbers are presented to be repeated in sequence, beginning with three and increasing to seven. This tests attention, concentration, memory and immediate recall.

PERFORMANCE SUBTESTS

1. Picture Completion

Pictures are presented with parts missing. For example, a pig without a tail, a face without a nose, and the child points to the missing part. This tests visual perception, and the ability to handle visual detail and separate foreground from background.

2. Picture Arrangement

Pictures are presented in a mixed-up order, child must arrange in sequence to tell a story. For example: child leaves home with school books, child meets other children walking to school, children cross the street at school patrol lane, teacher greets children in classroom. This tests not only the child's ability to follow visual sequence but also his capacity to reason cause and effect and to size up a total situation.

3. Block Design

Blocks are presented with different colors and designs on the sides; child must match design printed in book. This is another test of abstract abilities, how well the child can analyze and organize visual material. Visual perception and eye-hand coordination are important factors.

4. Object Assembly

Four large jigsaw puzzle pieces are presented, child must assemble them into a whole. This is another test of visual perception and organization, as well as eye-hand motor coordination.

5. Coding

Symbols are shown, each representing a number; child must transpose symbols, copying after associating with the proper number. This tests ability to understand a new problem and his visual-motor coordination to perform a task involving symbolization, an important factor in reading.

6. Mazes

The child must trace with a pencil through increasingly complicated mazes. Tests visual perception and hand-eye coordination.

When all the scores are tabulated, the examiner compares his findings with an established scale and reports the results in numbers, with a breakdown of how well the child did in each of his various subtests comparing his verbal abilities with his performance abilities. He thus obtains a "Verbal IQ," a "Performance IQ," and from these a "Full Scale IQ." This latter figure is the one generally used to express the single numerical IQ rating.

Just how accurate is such a test? Can we really assign a numerical figure like a baseball batting average to something as complicated and inadequately understood as intelligence? Is a child with an IQ of 122 actually more intelligent than a child who has one of 118? Is the IQ fixed for life or can it change by better teaching methods? And how much does the result depend upon the personal impressions or prejudices of the examiner? All of these questions have been raised, quite appropriately, by parents and teachers, and you can get a variety of answers depending upon the attitude of the particular individual with whom you are speaking. Being neither an educator nor a psychologist I will beg off from giving a specific answer except to say that to me it is obvious that a single IQ number, unless it is very low or very high, really tells me nothing about the child's capabilities, since the number usually reported is an *average* of a dozen different skills. One might as well say that Death Valley is an ideal place in which to live since the average temperature is 70 degrees F. — 140 during the day and zero at night!

And what does all of this have to do with the LD child? A proper evaluation first tells us that the learning-disabled is *not* truly retarded: he may actually achieve a rather high score in some of the subtests, whereas the child with mental deficiency shows low achievement all across the board. Next, the test reveals the "scatter" so characteristic of learning disability: instead of an even performance, we may find as much as a 20 to 30 point difference between the verbal score and performance score, with a marked variation in subtest rating. The tests considered most reliable in the verbal area are the ones on similarities and comprehension, while in the performance subtests the ones on coding and block design give us important clues about learning disability. Most important of all, a comprehensive study such as the WISC can guide remedial educational efforts by showing not only where the child's weaknesses exist, but where his strengths lie, so that a program can be built accordingly. How the teacher can use this information will be discussed again in Chapter 10.

There are many other tests that can be used as a clue to intelligence, and most examiners will prefer to use a number of different ones; what they call a battery of tests, in order to reach an accurate rating. If the child is too young or immature to cooperate properly, the examiner may use the Vineland Social Maturity test developed by Edgar Doll, in which the parent is asked a number of questions concerning the child's behavior and capabilities at home and in other situations. The child is not required to participate, and his level of intelligence is estimated by his developmental progress according to a scale of norms for such activities as pulling off his socks, marking with a crayon, and other similar activities. Depending upon the reliability of the informant, this test has a limited value when used for children too young to handle the WISC, which is usually considered most accurate for children from the ages of five or six to the teen-age level. Another test often used for additional information is the Peabody Picture Vocabulary Test, in which the child is asked to point to one of four pictures in response to the examiner's question (for example, "Show me the car"). This really tests the child's receptive vocabulary and not his general intelligence. Ammons and Ammons have developed a "Quick Test" which can be given in a much shorter time and is supposed to correlate well with the figures obtained on the WISC.

Most physicians are reluctant to trust their clinical judgment in borderline cases, but usually develop an impression of the intellectual progress and capabilities of the children they care for as they examine them at regular intervals. Some of the more severe causes of mental deficiency, such as PKU (phenylketonuria) or Down's Syndrome (mongolism) can be detected early and confirmed by well-established medical diagnostic studies. If a child is delayed in reaching such physical milestones as sitting alone or walking, or is especially slow in speech, his physician is alerted to be on the lookout for a possible intellectual deficiency. This last difficulty, a lag in verbal communication, has been commented upon by educators, who point out that any child who is not using speech to manipulate his environment by the age of three should be carefully observed for future learning difficulties. This observation, while correct, does not help us to spot most children with learning disabilities, especially the hyperactive ones whose parents report the child has been talking the ears off of any and all listeners since an early age.

It might be well to mention here once again that minimal brain dysfunction and specific learning disability are not synonymous terms, since it is possible for a child to have MBD and also be mentally retarded (or hard of hearing, or blue-eyed, or emotionally disturbed, or redheaded, and so forth), while *specific* learning disability excludes these other deficiencies. Hyperactivity and clumsiness, emotional instability and impulsivity, or other behavioral characteristics noted in the MBD child may be present in the retarded child as well, but the total incapacities of the retardate show in examination where his true difficulties lie. Management will depend not upon the diagnostic label attached to the child but upon the areas of his performance or deficiency that require attention.

Because of the overlap of behavioral characteristics, many professionals, including physicians, are still inclined to lump learning disabilities together with forms of mental deficiency. It was most discouraging to me to note that two of the newer and finer textbooks of pediatric neurology place learning disabilities and mental retardation in the same chapter. One even flatly asserts that most children who have learning difficulties have below average intelligence. Either someone is effectively screening out these children before we see them, or else our young population in Louisiana is markedly different from that of the rest of the country.

One of the complaints that Steve's mother, and many other mothers, have registered to me concerns the hush-hush attitude they encounter when attempting to find out how their children had performed on evaluation tests. There does indeed seem to be a conspiracy of silence among professionals in withholding information from interested parents. This is primarily based upon an inherent distrust of how well the parents will understand what they are told, and to what use they will put the results. Many parents have used IQ figures as a way to coerce their children into higher performance in school ("We know now that you could do better if you just tried harder"), or as a means of self-glorification in bragging to other parents about what brilliant children they have produced.

On the other end of the scale many parents have become despondent and even irrational in refusing to accept the realization that their child has performed below their expectations. Others will attempt to discover a means of coaching their child so that on a subsequent test he will know the answers ahead of time and thus perform more to their liking. Examiners have learned to their sorrow that these misunderstandings do occur and they attempt to prevent them by limiting what they tell parents, but parents still want to know. If I have a report of a child in hand, I try to explain to his parents the limitations of tests and, instead of quoting numerical figures, try to guide them to those individuals who are trained to use the test results as a basis for their remedial efforts.

Another criticism of our current intelligence tests is the fact that they depend so much on a child's own experiences and penalize the child who has not been given the same opportunities that others have. Instead of measuring his innate intelligence they more accurately reflect how much he has been exposed to in his environment that would help him learn. The rural child who has never been to a supermarket or waited at a traffic light, or the city child who has never fed a pig or milked a cow, is naturally not going to recognize these things as well as one who has. The child who has never been talked to or listened to is bound to do poorly on those tests relying on vocabulary and verbal skills. The child who has been deprived of experience or opportunity is not nearly so well prepared for school as he should be, as we mentioned several chapters back. However, one must be cautious before blaming all learning disabilities on socio-cultural deprivation and expecting that huge sums of money expended on programs designed to furnish enrichment will completely wipe out learning disabilities.

The inconsistency in performance of the learning-disabled child never ceases to amaze me. One child will be able to repeat everything that happened on a trip to Disneyland the previous summer, yet be unable to recall his school assignment from the previous day. Another may have handwriting so atrocious as to be almost illegible, and spelling so inconsistent as to be laughable were it not so disabling to him in the classroom, yet his mother may report that he can play a difficult game such as chess with unbelievable skill. It is easy to understand how a teacher or parent who has never encountered a child with learning disabilities and had his idiosyncrasies explained could readily feel that his classroom inabilities must reflect some sort of mental deficiency or lack of interest and motivation.

Two final notes of caution concerning testing: first, avoid at all costs over-testing the learning-disabled child. He is already anxious and concerned about himself, aware of his difficulties in the classroom and sensitive as all children with MBD are. It does not take him long to become aware of the significance of what is being done, so that continued or repeated testing can become a crushing blow to his self-esteem and morale, confirming his suspicions that there must be something seriously wrong with his brain, that he is indeed stupid or retarded or crazy, or even worse. Second, remember that testing and grading in school and on report cards are *not* accurate indications of a child's intelligence, motivation or effort, especially as concerns the child with learning disabilities. Overemphasis on the importance of obtaining better grades and punishment for not doing so can be his ruination. We will have much more to say about grades in subsequent chapters, but their effects on the learning-disabled child's self-opinion cannot be overemphasized.

6.

"HE HAS AN EMOTIONAL BLOCK"

The third misleader waves a banner with the suggestion that the learning-disabled child's problems have a psychological background, and are based upon his unfortunate experiences which have accumulated to such a level that they interfere with his thinking processes and thus obstruct his ability to learn in school. This concept has attracted an extensive following from those who are anxious to blame all of childhood's difficulties on poor environment, and who feel that parental mismanagement is the basic factor involved in all these ills. Since most of the courses in child psychology which teachers take during their training follow this line of reasoning, it is easy to understand why so many parents are told, as was Steve's mother, that the real fault lies in the home situation and only by skillful manipulation of the parents' roles can the problems be solved. Every book on child raising stresses the many wrongs that a mother can do, such as overprotection, neglect, domination, lack of concern, subconscious seduction — it's not difficult to find at least one thing that seems to need altering in any mother's attitude.

The classroom behavior of the LD child in the early grades follows the pattern that we mentioned in the discussion of minimal brain dysfunction. He is unable to sit still and follow directions, he is distractible and impulsive, and he is sensitive and cries readily when corrected or reprimanded, which he resents. All of this suggests to the teacher that he is a very immature child, who has been babied and overprotected by his mother. His low tolerance to frustration and his sulking attitude suggest that no one has ever said no to him, and that he has been thoroughly overindulged, or that no one has really been interested enough in him to teach him proper manners. Unless the teacher is familiar with the characteristics of MBD or has worked with other children having this problem, this is the only explanation that seems plausible to her. When the child fails to perform in his school work at the same level as his classmates, she decides that he is just not ready for school, and may fall back to the suggestions of our first two proponents: Leave him alone or see if perhaps he isn't just a bit retarded.

As the learning-disabled child continues in school, his problems become compounded. His inability to pay attention and concentrate, his difficulty in catching on to what is happening in the classroom, and his inability to put his knowledge down on paper all combine to hold back his level of classroom competency. As he looks about him and sees others doing with ease the things that he cannot seem to accomplish, his frustrations, which are already at a basically high level, reach the exploding point. His teacher, recognizing that he is capable of better performance, interprets all his misbehavior as indicative of his being a nervous child, and tells the parents that his emotions are blocking his learning process. When she recommends that the child see the school psychologist, he usually reports that the child is indeed experiencing emotional difficulty. The stage is then set for a long-term course of psychotherapy which is most often frustrating and humiliating to the parents who are told all the things they have done wrong to produce their child's problems, and even more upsetting to the child, since he is now convinced there is something basically wrong with himself. And when psychotherapy fails completely to help the child to learn to read or write or spell any better, as most often is the case, suggestions are made that perhaps there are deeper problems involved which require even more intensive — and expensive — sessions.

If the child and his parents then come under the care of a professional who intensely believes in the "dynamic" or "analytic" dogma of psychotherapy, their efforts become directed at uprooting and exposing the subconscious reasons why the child is not learning. Psychotherapists, basing their theories on the concept of disturbances in psychosexual development (the oral, anal, genital and latent stages they talk about), have advanced reasons, some quite outlandish, for a child's learning disorder. The following are examples.

1. Going to school is a child's first chance to get even with his parents, so he refuses to learn in order to punish them.

2. The child has deep sexual conflicts because he has been punished for peeking at his parents, so that the letters making up the words in his books look like sex organs and frighten him, blocking him from learning to read.

3. Along this same line, the child who has difficulty with geography is supposed to be disturbed because he associates "Mother Earth" with his own mother whom he was wrongly trying to get information about by il-

licitly stealing a look at her body, so that he feels guilty when he tries to find out about the world.

4. In attempting to explain why boys are found to have reading problems six to eight times more frequently than girls, the reason given is that the male is more aggressive sexually, and the female is passive, so that the male has more difficulty in suppressing the sexual aggression which blocks his learning capacities.

Fortunately, most of these theories have been thoroughly discredited as psychology and psychiatry are turning away from the strict orthodoxy of psychoanalysis. However, this school of thought has had a profound impact upon the training of our teachers and social workers and has left its mark indelibly upon their feelings toward children who misbehave. The intensity of its proponents is reminiscent of the religious fervor of the early evangelists, causing one observer to comment that reading about Freud and his followers reminded him of another great Jewish teacher who also attracted a group of followers, and that the Great Carpenter from Nazareth was fortunate to have been betrayed by only *one* disciple!

Not having been trained in psychology or psychiatry, I am unqualified to comment upon the treatment of adult emotional disorders, which perhaps do have a strong tendency toward psychosexual disturbances. But I have dealt with children for nearly twenty-five years, and I have yet to see a child who was having problems because he was in love with his mother and attracted to her sexually, this causing him to hate his father. Perhaps these instances do occur and are seen by professionals in child guidance or psychiatric clinics, but if this Oedipal conflict, which is described as occurring in almost everyone, were so common, it should be recognized by those of us who deal with all sorts of children day after day — and I have yet to find a pediatrician who has seen a case of this. The whole concept of analysis for children would appear to be on shaky grounds, yet the projective tests, such as the Rorschach ink-blot test, in which the observer interprets a deeper meaning from what the child says or does, are still discussed as being valid and accurate in working with children who have behavior problems. When I read these reports I am reminded of the story of the father who was hastily summoned to his child's kindergarten by his tearful wife who urged him to hurry because something dreadful had come up. Excusing himself from his work, he rushed out to find his five-year-old daughter sitting in the principal's office with his distraught wife and the school psychologist. "Mr. Jones," he was told firmly. "We fear your daughter has a deep-seated neurotic tendency. Look how she colors her pictures — all purple and black, the dark colors. This indicates a serious situation, and I am certain she needs psychotherapy immediately!" On the way home he tried to reassure his shaken wife by pointing how happy their daughter seemed, sitting on the back seat of the car, humming a little song to herself. As they were getting out of the car he asked, "Becky, honey, tell Daddy something — why did you color all your pictures purple and black?" " 'Cause, I broke all my other crayons!" was her reply as she ran off happily to play with her friends.

Before I bring the wrath of an entire profession down upon me, let me hasten to state that all school psychologists are not so authoritative, and the concept of minimal brain dysfunction is becoming accepted as a much more rational explanation for the problems of learning-disabled children. Workers are beginning to decide that all children do not come into the world with a basic hatred of their parents, that all parents do not reject their children deep down inside, and that it is possible for decent, loving parents, who are concerned about their children and genuinely interested in their progress in school, to have children who behave in a manner unacceptable to the school authorities. When this aberrant behavior is accompanied by difficulties in the communicating skills, the possibility of specific learning disabilities is now strongly considered. When the teacher or counselor sits down with the parents and explains this disorder in a rational manner, not only does it relieve the parents of a tremendous load of guilt, but also it removes a great deal of responsibility from the teacher and the school system in the parents' minds, since they are much more inclined to blame the school, especially if they have been sincere in their efforts to understand and help their child. An attitude of mutual cooperation can be achieved, often for the first time, when the parents come to realize that the problem is due to a basic biochemical difficulty rather than willful disobedience on the part of their child, their own mismanagement, or ineptness on the part of his teachers.

The concept of specific learning disability based on a biochemical imbalance associated with a dysfunction of the nervous system could not have been fully understood and appreciated until the advent of corrective medication. Only when, after receiving proper medication, the child shows striking improvement in all of his behavioral difficulties — in self-control, organization in the classroom, concentration, willingness to do his school work — can those about him recognize the true nature of his disorder and remove from him the stigma associated with emotional disturbance.

Not that the LD child does not have emotional problems. If he is allowed to go along without help until he is in the upper elementary grades or junior high school level, then his behavior becomes so disturbed, due to day after day of embarrassment and humiliation and week after week of rejection by his teacher and his classmates, that the emotional overlay is extremely intense, and it completely overshadows his learning disorder. He then definitely needs counselling and emotional support. Otherwise his misdeeds may soon attract the attention not only of his teacher or school principal but also of the correctional authorities as well, and his unfortunate record as a troublemaker may move from the school's files to the police blotter. Sympathetic juvenile officers are beginning to go back into offenders' academic histories and tie in the lack of school achievement with the basic underlying cause of their behavior problems.

Workers dealing with adolescents and young adults who have a long history of learning difficulties find that the most important facet of the problem that must be dealt with is not the educational handicap but the low self-esteem and lack of confidence which have resulted from years of humiliating school failure. Only by stressing the necessity for successful achievements and a strong program of supportive reassurance can these unfortunate individuals be helped, but for many this comes too late to be really beneficial. If ever the old adage of "an ounce of prevention" applied, it is in this important area of concern for the learning-disabled.

7.

"SEE IF HE HAS BRAIN DAMAGE"

Our next misguider suggests that the learning-disabled child has had some form of injury to his brain, most likely during the birth process, which causes him to behave and perform the way he does, and that in order to understand him and treat him properly we must locate the area in his brain where this damage has occurred and find out exactly how it happened. That certain accidents during the newborn (neonatal) period can result in the more obvious disorders of childhood such as cerebral palsy has been well established through the efforts of the great pioneer pediatric neurologist, Meyer Perlstein. He described those conditions which cause hemorrhage into the brain, such as difficult delivery, Caesarean section, and premature birth, as well as those conditions in which the brain is deprived of oxygen (anoxia) during the crucial first moments of life, such as when there is a breech delivery, a cord wrapped around the neck, or excessive sedation to the mother. He found a high correlation between hemorrhagic damage and spastic cerebral palsy, and between anoxic conditions and the athetoid form of cerebral palsy, in which the incoordination of movements is the primary finding. By examining the brains of the infants who died shortly after birth he was able to find evidence to support his conclusions, and by following those infants who survived beyond the newborn period he was able, with a high degree of accuracy, to relate the birth history with the resultant neurological disorder. He also noted the relationship of cerebral palsy to the other disorders of childhood such as mental retardation and epilepsy, and paved the way for the studies of Denhoff on brain dysfunction which we mentioned in Chapter 1, and which are illustrated in Figure 1.

The idea of birth injury and brain damage to the infant is so firmly fixed in the minds of most of those who work with children with behavior or learning disorders that it is almost impossible to eliminate it. The classical publications of Alfred Strauss entitled *Psychopathology and Education of the Brain-Injured Child* became the Bible for all those concerned with the learning-disabled. They described the behavior and learning problems in connection with difficulties in attention and perception which we now recognize and associate with MBD, yet Dr. Strauss himself told me how he regretted the fact that the term minimal brain damage had become so solidly entrenched. To label a child as being brain-damaged sounds to most people as if he were the village idiot, and the learning-disabled child is far from that. As others observed these children, the concept of minimal brain damage was developed. It proposed that all children had some degree of injury to the brain during the birth process and that those infants who were more severely injured would fail to survive, while those who were less affected might live but develop cerebral palsy. Those whose brain injury was only minimal would escape apparent damage in the newborn period, however might turn up later with behavioral disorders or learning problems. A specific study on reading disorders was made in 1959 in which the birth certificates of 372 children with reading disabilities, referred from the Baltimore public schools, were consulted. The conclusions reached indicated a significantly higher incidence of birth complications and maternal bleeding during pregnancy for the injured children.

With all the weight of this evidence it would seem foolhardy to doubt the proposition of False Prophet Number Four. However, as we become more involved and see more children with learning disabilities, there are several factors that stand out as not fitting so neatly into the brain-damage concept, and they have made me wonder about its overall reliability. First, there is the matter of the overwhelming preponderance of *boys* involved, nearly six to eight times as many males are cited in almost every report, by the British pioneers, by Orton and in present-day studies. Even the Baltimore researchers admitted they elected to do their study on boys only since they could not find enough girls to give their study statistical significance. I realize that the male infant is reputed to be the weaker of the two sexes and is perhaps more vulnerable to injury in the newborn period, but the ratio is just too one-sided to make this a valid reason. Second is the striking increased incidence of learning disorders in certain families. These families may have two or three children with learning disabilities, and careful questioning usually reveals that one or more of the parents or grandparents also had problems in school. Sometimes this information is not too easy to evaluate, since learning difficulties are not a matter of familial pride, but when a parent tells me her son's grandfather quit school in the sixth grade so he could help out on the farm, or left high school because he wanted to go to work, I always wonder what the real reason was for his leaving school.

Many times the history can be confusing. A mother whom I saw recently told me she knew her child's difficulty was the result of her excessive smoking during pregnancy. She related how she had been a chain smoker when first married, but after having a miscarriage she consulted an obstetrician who told her that if she wanted to get pregnant and have a normal child she should give up smoking completely. So she did, according to her story, and, some time after, she conceived and carried a child to term without mishap. She then related how she went back to smoking and some three years later had another child. This was the one that she had brought to our office because of learning and behavior difficulties — the child had a short attention span, and was distractible, unable to concentrate and complete school assignments, and was very poor in reading, writing and spelling. The child's examination revealed many of the characteristics of MBD: confused laterality, poor digit identification and very distorted handwriting. We discussed the possible harmful effects of smoking on the developing baby, since there have been reports indicating that smoking may be harmful, but when I began to mention how frequently we found this disorder in a familial situation, she looked at me in surprise, and then said, "Doctor, I'm going to tell you something I've never told anyone before. The night I got my high school diploma, I went home and cried. I knew I hadn't really learned enough in school to justify graduating, but I knew how to behave and not annoy teachers, so they always passed me. And do you know — I can see so much of me in my child!" I concluded our interview with one more question, "Do you think *your* mother smoked heavily when she was carrying you?"

Another puzzling aspect that casts some doubt on the question as to whether or not these children are really brain-damaged is their response to medication. The brain contains some eighteen billion nerve cells which are so highly developed in special function that whenever one is destroyed it cannot reproduce itself, as many other cells in the body can, but is replaced by scar tissue. If the behavior and academic problems of the learning-disabled child are indeed the result of brain damage, then these cells have been injured beyond repair, and no medication could produce such spectacular improvement. It is true that we use only a fraction of the total number of brain cells we have, and perhaps could learn to use the dormant ones to take over the function of damaged ones, but the rapid change in behavior and classroom performance under proper medication would tend to discount any actual structural basis for the problem and point to a biochemical basis for the disorder.

The insistence upon a structural basis to account for the problems of learning-disabled children has held back many physicians from accepting the idea of brain dysfunction and kept them believing that most of these patients do indeed have brain damage. Throughout his medical training the physician is taught that all the ailments to which the human body falls heir can be divided into two categories: organic and functional. The term organic is synonymous with structural or physical. When a patient is presented to his physician with a complaint that can be tied in with something specific the doctor can find in an examination, such as an elevated white blood count, an obviously reddened and inflamed ear drum, a heart murmur, or a change in an X-ray picture, he can readily assume that this is a real illness. He can prove there is an alteration in anatomical structure, and tries to discover from the patient's history just what caused this disruption so that he can treat the patient by removing the offending agent. If his patient is so ill that he requires hospitalization, upon discharge, the physician must complete his patient's chart by recording the diagnosis which can be coded numerically according to adopted standards in two units. One is for the location of the disease, the second for the cause of the illness. If he is unable to satisfactorily determine the location and cause, the physician is apt to think that the patient's problem is functional, which is another word for psychosomatic or emotional. The physician has transmitted to other professions this kind of division, so that many of the tests used by the psychologists and other evaluators lean heavily upon the idea that they must show the presence of organicity in an attempt to rule out psychogenic causes for the child's learning problems. One such test developed by Lauretta Bender is the Bender Visual Motor Gestalt test, in which the child is asked to reproduce a series of figures, largely geometric. The examiner then interprets according to how well the child performs. This test has been widely accepted and is almost standard in any evaluation of children with learning or behavior disorders. It is supposed to reflect the eye-hand coordination of the child, and his ability to properly handle the test's tasks is interpreted as suggesting the presence of brain damage. Another test frequently used is the Goodenough Draw-a-Man test, in which the child is asked to draw a picture of a man, or a person, or himself. This test is thought to indicate not only visual memory and eye-hand coordination but also the child's own body image. This has been expanded to the Person-House-Tree drawing test which is interpreted in the same manner. At one time or another I have used all of these in the office but I have not personally felt that they can really be used to indicate damage to the brain. I now feel that I can obtain much more information of practical value to classroom application by asking the child to write me a note, and then studying his handwriting, his spelling, and what he is trying to tell me.

Another test which many have believed indicated the presence of brain damage is the electroencephalogram, or the EEG. Since the German physiologist Hans Berger first demonstrated in 1928 that he could attach wires to the scalp and amplify the electrical current generated on the surface of the brain enough to make a tracing, scientists have been studying these brain waves and attempting to relate them both to function and to disease processes. The most striking variations in the EEG tracing are seen in patients who are prone to seizures. The usual regular rhythms are disturbed by sharp spikes or spikes and waves of a different nature. Maturity produces specific changes, the adult picture being much better organized than that of the infant and young child, so that even in experienced hands the interpretation of a child's EEG may vary considerably. Some electroencephalographers demand much more specific alterations before they will report an EEG as being abnormal, while others tend to overread them and attach more significance than they should to minor variations. I have even seen an EEG reported as "indicative of a learning disorder," which is of course absurd and impossible, since learning difficulty is an educational problem and not an electrical disturbance.

Attempts to study the true value of the EEG have produced conflicting results. One recent study at Johns Hopkins reported that nearly fifty percent of all the children referred to their clinic for learning disabilities showed abnormalities on the EEG and concluded that this was a valuable diagnostic tool. I read over this report, and then re-read it, because to me it also said fifty percent of the children *didn't* have abnormalities, and nearly thirty percent of the children without learning problems that were used as controls in this study had the same vague abnormalities reported. Since the EEG measures the electrical activity on the surface of the cortex of the brain, and since the disorder in MBD appears to be a biochemical disturbance deep in the base of the brain or the brain stem, we can now understand why the EEG has been a disappointing tool in the study of MBD children. But many interested people who work with learning-disabled children are convinced that this test must be done, and I have even known teachers to insist to parents that they have an EEG run on their child. Everyone has seen the astronauts on television with the wires leading to their scalps, so being attached to this machine is no longer frightening. Perhaps this is because it is a machine;

and in these modern days we have an unholy awe for what machines can do. We buy exercise machines and weight-reducing machines, and how many detective thrillers have the suspect undergo a lie-detector test in which the almighty machine is supposed to tell us whether or not the individual is guilty or innocent. Just as there is no machine to which we can hook up a person and have it tell us absolutely whether or not he is telling the truth, so we don't have one to which we can attach a child and have it say, "You're five foot two, with eyes of blue, and you have brain damage." Sometimes I will request a tracing for a child whose parents are overly insistent, or for a child who has frequent episodes of loss of consciousness accompanied by staring spells which suggest a petit mal epilepsy, a rather rare disorder of childhood. But for most of my learning-disabled children I am inclined to agree with the pediatric neurologist Sidney Carter who advised the mothers of his patients to take the thirty-five or forty dollars that a test would cost and buy a new hat, since this would do the child as much good as the EEG and make the mother feel much better!

There is one new development currently being investigated, using the EEG, which has aroused considerable interest among researchers who are attempting to devise a more objective method of diagnosing MBD. They have noted that, when a child is exposed to carefully controlled timed flashes of light, a response in the brain wave is produced after an interval of time which is different for the child with MBD. These responses are referred to as "evoked potentials," and they can be measured very accurately by use of a computer. At the present time, the practical application of this test is limited because of the expense involved and the scarcity of the necessary equipment. However, the investigators working in this area hope that they will be able to develop a more positive test for MBD which would eliminate the current criticism that so many of the psychological and educational tests are biased against those children who have not had sufficient educational opportunities.

No discussion concerning brain damage and learning disorders would be complete without some reference to cerebral hemisphere dominance and mixed laterality, since this too is an area of widespread misunderstanding. As we have seen (in Figure 6), the brain is divided into the cerebrum or upper portions, the cerebellum, and the various portions of the sub-brain and brain stem. The cerebrum is divided into two hemispheres, left and right. Since the pathways which carry the impulses of sensation from the body up to the brain and those which carry the currents of movements and activity from the brain down to the body cross from one side to the other, the left hemisphere controls the right side of the body and the right the left side of the body. Man is the only animal known to develop handedness, a strong inclination to use one hand in preference to the other in performing skilled acts. The hemisphere that controls the preferred side is called the dominant hemisphere, and it is usually the left, since over ninety percent of all adult humans are right-handed. The establishment of preference and handedness is part of development, since most infants appear to use either hand with equal ease. By two years of age, however, they usually begin to show some degree of preference, although handedness may not become firmly established for another four or five years. Delay in developmental maturity, such as is seen in MBD, can manifest itself by delay in strong hand preference, so that the child who has reached school age without demonstrating a firm laterality preference should arouse suspicion of this problem. Usually the lack of established handedness is accompanied by motor incoordination and awkwardness. When a parent says his child is ambidextrous he often really means "ambi-clumsy," for the child may not really use either hand well. Since studies of brain localization are all based upon observation of adults, it is unwise to assume that similar specific areas have been firmly established in an immature brain which is undergoing development. The adult who has a center or centers for speech in his dominant hemisphere may lose his ability to talk if he has a stroke or other injury involving that side of his brain. But there are no areas in the child's brain that are specifically reading centers or math centers which could be damaged and affect these skills in an isolated manner.

The relationship between gross and fine motor incoordination and MBD we have mentioned before, and it is striking enough to have aroused a great deal of interest on the part of Orton in his original works on reading problems. He questioned whether or not the hemisphere of the brain might be faulty when firm dominance was not established, and wondered what could be done to improve this condition. He noted the tendency of many of the children with reading problems to show mirror-writing and reading reversals, and suggested that these difficulties might be due to reversed "engrams," impressions on the nerve cells which developed backwards in the opposite or wrong hemisphere. He also reported on the incidence of mixed dominance in which the child would prefer the right hand and the left eye, or left hand and right foot. In his later writings, however, Orton stressed that he found most of his reading-disabled children were right-handed, right-eyed, and right-footed and that it was wrong to associate handedness and reading disability too closely. But the notion that mixed dominance was a sign of brain damage had already been firmly established, so that every case study of a learning-disabled child includes a statement concerning his laterality preference.

And preference it must be, since we have no conclusive evidence to indicate that in the child one hemisphere dominates over the other one, and that training to strengthen the supposedly dormant side of the brain will improve his reading. Nevertheless, prolonged exercises and other measures such as restraining one arm and patching one eye have been used. The fallacy of the eye patch can readily be appreciated if we simply examine the anatomy and function of the visual system (Figure 9), since the right eye is not controlled by the left side of the brain, or vice versa, but each eye receives part of the visual field and transmits the image back to the brain through a partial crossing of the fibers of the optic nerve. Patching the eye may produce apparent temporary improvement if the eye muscles are considerably imbalanced. Removing the image received from one eye may eliminate double vision, but as soon as the patch is removed the child is back where he started. Other exercise programs which take the child back through crawling in

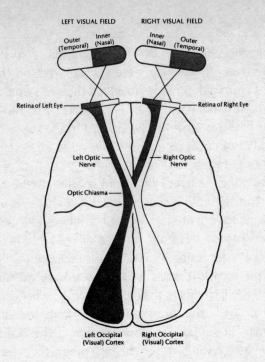

Figure 9. Transmission and Reception of Visual Fields in the Brain

In this diagrammatic figure the brain is visualized from above. The impulses from the outer (temporal) portion of each visual field are received on the inner portion of the retina of the corresponding eye, while the inner (nasal) portion falls upon the outer portion of each retina. The retinal fibers pass back to form the left and right optic nerves, each carrying a portion of the visual image as shown. The two optic nerves come together at the optic chiasma where a partial crossing of the fibers occurs, with the images from the left inner and right outer visual fields being transmitted back to the cortex of the left occipital lobe, while the right occipital lobe receives the visual image of the left outer and right inner fields. This demonstrates how patching an eye to block out the reception of vision by that one eye would reduce half the visual impulses received by each occipital cortex, and would do nothing to strengthen or make more dominant the opposite hemisphere.

an effort supposed to reproduce a normal progression of neural organization are equally invalid, since a number of excellent readers are reported by their parents to have skipped the crawling stage, while many poor readers are stated to have gone through this stage without difficulty.

Actually the entire field of the relationship between motor skills and learning disorders needs much greater clarification if we are to utilize our knowledge properly. Although delay in the achievement of milestones of physical activity such as sitting, standing, and walking have been noted in respect to actual mental deficiency, there is certainly no correlation in the other direction. In my senior year at Byrd High School our football team won the Louisiana State championship, and our starting backfield contained four marvelously skilled and coordinated athletes; however, I had classes with them, and, believe me, none of them would be considered as great students or superior intellects. As a television fan of ice hockey, I watch in awe as these giants skate back and forth across the ice, showing unbelievable coordination and splendid reflex abilities. But I feel certain that none of these gentlemen, while being reasonably intelligent, would want to claim outstanding scholastic ability purely on the basis of their great physical talents. I was so clumsy (and still am) that I never could learn to ride a bicycle well, quit going to skating parties because I was too embarrassed to have all the other children watch me fall down, and finally learned to swim as an adult so my children wouldn't drown when we took them swimming. Yet my family had me reading by the time I was four and a half, so that I was able to enter school at five and even skipped to the second grade. Interestingly enough, I always blamed my poor handwriting on the fact that I had to learn writing by staying after school in the second grade, but now I realize this, together with my lack of coordination, constitutes my share of MBD.

Does that mean that my brain is structurally different and that by careful microscopic analysis of my brain tissue some pathologist could determine that I was clumsy, but enjoyed reading? Is there an anatomical basis for the fact that some people prefer vanilla to chocolate, or that some can tinker with motors and repair anything, while others like myself can't even drive a nail straight? I doubt that the presence or absence of a certain skill demands a specific structural configuration in the way an individual's brain is built. This lack of specific anatomical localization makes looking for the part of the brain that is damaged or defective in a dyslexic child a rather fruitless task.

As we said before, every child with brain dysfunction does not necessarily have a learning disorder, nor does every child with learning disability have to be awkward or poorly coordinated; *all* of them do not need a motor-training program. The MBD child who is clumsy may enjoy jumping on a trampoline, walking a balance board and rolling and tumbling, since it may give him more assurance and awareness of his own body, but I have my doubts as to whether it will help him be a better reader. For the learning-disabled child who is well coordinated, assignment to such a program is not only unnecessary but soon becomes boring and another source of annoyance and frustration. Just as each learning-disabled child needs an individualized educational program tailored to his own requirements, he also should be managed according to his own motor skills or difficulties.

In conclusion we should comment on the possible relationship between an unfavorable environment for the child and the production of brain damage. In Figure 2 we outlined the relative importance of opportunity and experience in the progression of the child to the state of developmental maturity. In Figure 3 we suggested that the lack of such opportunity and experience, because of what is called socio-cultural deprivation, might interfere with the necessary feedback required to achieve normal progression, thus causing the child to remain developmentally immature. Children who are hospitalized excessively during their early life or who are institutionalized in a setting in which they are deprived of a normal warm human relationship do indeed lag behind in achieving developmental milestones, but whether this can actually produce damage to the brain is still an unanswered question. In a similar vein, those children who are deprived of normal nutrition during their formative months are felt to be likely to develop brain damage. In relation to this, it has been shown that in experimental animals such as rats, malnutrition can definitely affect learning abilities. These testings have not been adequately duplicated for humans, and while all of us look forward to the day when no child shall go hungry in a world of plenty, it seems likely that even on that golden day learning disabilities will still be with us.

My private practice has been with average middle-class children in a Southern city of nearly two hundred thousand, and, while I cannot be absolutely certain, I do feel that most of my patients have not been severely malnourished. The rest of my experience with learning-disabled children has come from the neurology clinic conducted under the Louisiana State Department of Crippled Children, where we see children not only from our city but also from the surrounding nine-parish rural areas as well. I have been able to detect little difference between my private patients and clinic patients either in history, or physical findings, or in the types of their learning difficulties. Our state clinic patients perhaps do not reflect a true picture of the general population since their parents are interested enough to bring them in and follow through with the medication and our remedial recommendations. When other physicians become involved in helping the learning-disabled child and begin to report their observations, we will be able to settle the question of brain damage more correctly. My impression is that, instead of considering the likely probability that an inherited, biochemical disorder is the basis of MBD and the resultant learning disabilities, we have been placing too much emphasis on the importance of the history of neonatal stress and its consequences. We should certainly continue to improve our facilities for treatment of the newborn and increase our diagnostic skills in observing them. However, to suggest to the parents that their child is a high risk for learning disorders, or that a child without brain damage from a birth injury does not have a learning disability, but that his difficulty is the result of an unfavorable environment, appears unwarranted in the light of my experience and that of others. There may well be a combination of factors, and an hereditary predisposition which renders a child more vulnerable to injury to his nervous system, but only additional research can help us determine this. The proper kind of research is going to be rather difficult for those concerned with dyslexia, for at the present time we have no experimental animals who can read and write.

8.

"LET'S GO BACK TO GOOD OLD PHONICS"

This is the slogan of our next blind man who has attracted quite a large following by suggesting that children never would have had reading problems if *those people* hadn't come along and meddled with our school system with their progressive ideas, and that all we need to do to solve all of our children's problems is to go back to phonics and teach them just as we did in the good old days. All this talk about dyslexia is just a lot of imaginary confusion, they contend, because there just wasn't any such thing until educators started using the "look-say" method of teaching reading instead of the ABC's they remember in McGuffey's primers. Rallying behind the misinformation contained in a popular best-seller of the thirties which told them why Johnny couldn't read, the phonics enthusiasts still carry a lot of weight in scholastic circles where the problems of the learning-disabled child are considered to have an educational basis exclusively. Even today some of the very latest publications by respected authors fail to take notice of the differences in the language skills of individual children, and continue to recommend a unilateral approach to solving their learning problems.

What about the look-say method and all the terrible things for which it has been blamed? The reason that the look-say technique became popular with educators who were hoping to help more children learn to read faster and better is that it is actually the manner in which a skilled reader accomplishes his task. He does not stop to analyze each single letter or syllable but recognizes and reproduces the whole word just as he recognizes the familiar face of an old friend. He does not need to look at each eye, then the nose, then the mouth, then the ears, but puts them all together at once to identify his friend. This putting together of different parts is what the psychologists refer to as the Gestalt method, in which recognition of the entire unit occurs. In the classroom the child who does not have a learning disability can begin with whole words, first associating them with the pictures in the books that he has, then later recognizing them without the picture. He learns to visualize the object the word is supposed to represent in his mind's eye without reading the picture clue, and remembers how the word sounded in his mind's ear so that he is able to reproduce it verbally. From the flash cards which had only the word to be recognized, the capable reader could proceed to acquire a more extensive vocabulary of "sight-words." The words were then associated with meaning, and were linked together into phrases and finally sentences to express complete ideas. The child who had already learned some technique in the handling of grammar, tenses, and syntax through his early language development now begins to associate the printed symbols with the known object. The child without dyslexia can readily master the look-say method, and in most instances will find it a satisfactory manner in which to learn reading.

The main objection I have heard from educators —

and from my own children — is that the books printed for beginning look-say readers have a restricted vocabulary, since they must be limited to only those words which have been taught — how many different ways can you say "Look, Jane, look. See Spot run. Run, Spot, run"? The good reader with an inquisitive mind soon became bored with the same old words and the same old sentences and yearned to break out of the restraints that limited his search for knowledge. However, he soon began to devise ways to figure out new words on his own and in most instances did not find look-say a drawback in his progression to higher language skills.

And what of phonics? Is the old ABC breakdown and gradual building of units into words really that much better? As I am not an educator, allow me to decline getting involved in this perennial argument, but it appears to me that for the average reader it really doesn't seem to make a great deal of difference how he is taught. Since reading involves the blending of visual and auditory skills in using and reproducing printed symbols, which at least eighty percent of our school population appear to be able to do with ease, either technique in the hands of a good teacher will accomplish the desired result. Actually, few teachers ever teach without using some phonics, for every time they read a story to their pupils and call their attention to how the words were pronounced, or read a nursery rhyme which taught them sound-alikes, or give a lesson in spelling which stressed the sounds of letters or combinations, they use phonics. The child learns to associate the sound units (phonemes) with their written counterparts (graphemes) and thus develops the ability to write down these graphic symbols to express his ideas.

What about the learning-disabled child? As we mentioned before, his disorganization does not permit the skillful blending and proper processing of auditory and visual stimuli and interferes when he attempts to reproduce them. Recalling the Myklebust-Boder findings described in Chapter 3, we can appreciate the fact that a large group of dyslexic children (nearly sixty percent) fall into the group who are stronger visually than auditorily, so going back to good old phonics is just what he *doesn't* need. This is the reason that any program based upon one single concept for the correction of the reading difficulties of all children is doomed to failure. For the fifteen to twenty percent who are stronger in auditory than in visual function, the look-say method may prove to be a blessing in disguise, since it calls attention to their problems much earlier and should alert the teacher to their need for special attention.

Since the problems of the learning-disabled child may be complex and often confusing, most authorities agree that a thorough and comprehensive evaluation is desirable in order to choose the best remedial methods to be used. The one test that is generally considered to be the most reliable is the Illinois Test of Psycholinguistic Abilities, abbreviated ITPA, developed in 1961 by Samuel Kirk and James McCarthy at the University of Illinois, and recently (in 1968) revised into its present form. The authors consider the test a diagnostic rather than a classificatory tool, and note that it differs from the usual reading test in that it measures specific abilities and difficulties in communicating skills rather than overall reading ability according to grade level. In this respect it resembles the WISC (see Chapter 5) which breaks down specific areas in intellectual functioning, and it actually has some ingredients which are very similar to the WISC. Composed of twelve subtests, the ITPA attempts to evaluate the levels of language input, organization and output (compare with Figure 5) in the following manner.

Subtest 1. *Auditory Reception*

(formerly called auditory decoding) The child answers yes or no to questions such as "Do birds fly?" "Do rocks eat?" "Do cats sing?" This tests ability to understand the spoken word.

Subtest 2. *Visual Reception*

(formerly called visual decoding) A picture of a horse is presented — child is told to find horse from series of pictures of child, man, horse, bird. Tests ability to gain meaning from visual symbols, and to some extent visual memory, since the original key picture is removed before the four comparison pictures are shown.

Subtest 3. *Visual Sequential Memory*

(formerly called visual-motor sequencing) Chips with designs are shown to the child, who must duplicate the design on a tray. Tests ability to reproduce sequence of non-meaningful visual figures, thus checking immediate rote memory.

SUBTEST 4. *Auditory Association*

(formerly called auditory vocal association) A verbal analogy is given which the child must complete, such as, "The sky is blue, snow is _____." "A dog is big, a puppy is _____." Tests ability to "relate spoken words in a meaningful way." This subtest is supposed to have a high correlation with the mental age.

SUBTEST 5. *Auditory Sequential Memory*

A sequence of numbers (digits) must be repeated. Tests ability to reproduce verbal sequence and immediate auditory recall.

SUBTEST 6. *Visual Association*

(formerly called visual-motor association) A group of five pictures is presented, a central one surrounded by four on the outside. The child must pick the outer picture which goes most closely with the central one. Tests ability to relate concept presented visually.

SUBTEST 7. *Visual Closure*

The child is shown picture of single cat, then is presented a larger picture and asked, "Show me another cat. Find all the cats." Tests ability to relate object from incomplete visual presentation.

SUBTEST 8. *Verbal Expression*

(formerly called encoding) The child is shown five different objects, such as a pencil, a sugar cube, a hammer, and asked, "Tell me all about this." Tests ability to express own concepts verbally.

SUBTEST 9. *Grammatic Closure*

(formerly called auditory-vocal closure) The child is told incomplete statement accompanied by a picture, such as, "Here is a horse; here are two _____." Tests automatic habits in use of grammar and syntax.

SUBTEST 10. *Manual Expression*

The child is given toy drum and asked, "Show me what we do with this." Tests ability to express ideas with gestures.

SUBTEST 11. *Auditory Closure*

Words are presented with sounds omitted such as, "moth-_____," "____ootball." Tests ability to fill in missing parts of words.

SUBTEST 12. *Sound Blending*

The child is presented individual sounds of a word ("quh" "uh" "mmm," for g-u-m) and must give complete word. Tests ability to construct a whole word from the composite sounds.

From the information thus obtained the examiner has evaluated the receptive or decoding processes (subtests 1 and 2), the organizing or associative processes (subtests 4 and 6), the expressive or encoding processes (subtests 8 and 10), and at the automatic level the closure processes (subtests 7, 9, 11 and 12) and sequential memory processes (subtests 3 and 5). Utilizing this information he can develop a specific remedial prescription for each individual child.

As with the WISC, this material as presented is not intended to be used by anyone for diagnostic testing, since the actual test is much more complete. But it is presented to emphasize once again how intricate and complicated the communicating skills are and how no one cure-all will ever work for every learning-disabled child. Most examiners will use the ITPA as one of a battery of tests, which may include the Wide Range Achievement Test (WRAT) or the Gray Oral Reading Tests, to measure actual reading performance, and the Frostig Developmental Test of Visual Perception and the Wepman Auditory Discrimination Test, to evaluate visual and auditory functions.

Other reasons have been given by the "all we need to do-ers" to explain the learning problems of our children, most of which try to put the blame on factors in the environment which have to do with language skills. One hears frequently that the real difficulty is the English language itself, because it is such an un-phonetic tongue. The great playwright George Bernard Shaw, a strong advocate of changing the spelling to more accurately reflect the true sounds of words, once challenged his audience to pronounce GHOTI. After receiving a number of varying answers, he announced the correct way was "fish": gh as in tough, o as in women, and ti as in nation. Some of the peculiarities of English do indeed confuse learning-disabled children, but these children have "cousins" in nearly all the foreign lands. Macdonald Critchley, speaking at the National Conference on Dyslexia in 1966, said that he had seen patients who were dyslexic in Portuguese, a highly phonetic written language, as well as in all the other Latin tongues, in Arabic, which is written and read from right to left, and in Japanese. Interestingly enough, I have a report concerning Japanese children which points out that there are two kinds of Japanese scripts. One resembles picture-writing and the children who use it are rarely dyslexic. The other symbolizes sounds, and reading disability does occur in its use. Another corrective technique used for reading difficulties is the ITA, or Initial Teaching Alphabet, which tries to overcome the problems produced by the differences between English spelling and pronunciation. It uses forty-four sound symbols to replace the usual English letters. A special typewriter is required, as are special books, but many teachers have found this a valuable method of getting the child started on a successful reading program.

Other reasons for poor reading performance have been advanced by the "go-backers," blaming crowded school-rooms, poorly trained teachers, or overanxious parents who push their children too hard. None of these seem valid when we note that a good number of children learn to read consistently in spite of these adverse influences. The learning-disabled children I have encountered have turned up in small, middle-sized, and large classrooms, under good, bad and indifferent teachers, and the over-anxiety I have noted in most of the parents of my patients comes from the fact that they realize that their children are not able to keep up with the other children in their same classroom.

The question of the effect of a bilingual household, in which the parents speak a foreign tongue while sending their children to school to learn English, has been raised as a possible deterrent to the children's learning to read. Certainly the child with MBD who is already disorganized will be further confused in this situation, but there are too many fine readers and excellent speakers who grew up in such a situation, for example on the lower East Side of New York City when it was a real melting-pot, to allow us to consider this a primary cause of reading disorders. Lately there has been increasing concern that many children who do not hear proper English at home come to school and cannot understand the teacher, since they have never heard anyone speak as she does. The suggestion has been made that the teachers must learn their jargon language so that they can better communicate with these children, and that they must teach in this distorted English rather than show them correct diction and grammar. Personally, this entire idea disturbs me greatly, since these children will find that most of the books from which they can learn are printed in "real" English, and most of the people in the outside world with whom they must learn to deal if they are to advance and succeed, speak proper English. Special attention should certainly be given to these children and their individual and collective needs, but I cannot understand how lowering the teacher's language performance is going to elevate that of the children under her care.

9.

"DON'T PUT THAT CHILD ON DRUGS!"

Our last false prophet brandishes a slogan that has stirred up one of the most impassioned controversies in recent medical history. It has caused so much confusion that the educational and medical professions as well as the general public are markedly divided in opinion concerning this important aspect of the management of the LD child. Since at the present time the proper use of medication appears to constitute a significant adjunct to remedial education by bringing long-awaited help to the child with classroom difficulties associated with MBD, it is important to study as objectively as possible the criticisms voiced by the opposition group and set the record straight once and for all concerning this highly volatile issue.

Launching a campaign so bitter and vicious that it nearly ended the work of one Midwestern pediatrician who had observed, as so many of us have, the beneficial effects of medication for LD children, the protestors received a welcome ear from the more sensational journalists who wrote scathing editorials in their newspapers or appeared on national television to condemn the abhorrent practice of "drugging" children in the classroom. Just as the opponents of fluoridation of the public water supplies were often able to block the effective use of that public health measure by using scare tactics and misinformation, these self-appointed crusaders hinted at the existence of some sort of sinister plot, perhaps Communistic, to gain control of our children by the use of what they called "mind-tampering drugs." They suggested there was collusion between the teaching and medical profession to narcotize into submission those children who annoyed their teachers by misbehaving and acting up in the classroom, implying that if the teachers were better qualified and more skilled in disciplinary management of these "normally exuberant" youngsters, they would not have to resort to drugs. The clamor they raised had many ramifications, causing even the usually conservative *Saturday Review* to publish an article (in their November 21, 1970 issue) entitled "Pills for Classroom Peace?" which they headlined across the front cover of that issue in large red print. By tying in with the national concern over the current drug problem these protestors finally were able to secure a Congressional investigation into the matter, affording a platform for those who felt "to cow little children into insensibility and silence by the administration of mind-dulling drugs is an unescapable obscenity and a perversion of every value that most Americans hold sacred."

Certainly anyone who would find fault with that statement, which appeared in the transcript of the committee's proceedings, must be against motherhood and apple pie, but what are the true facts of the situation? Are these drugs truly dangerous? Are they habit-forming, so that they are causing us to raise a generation of addicts? Do they cover up the *real* causes of learning difficulties, which many believe to be poor parental care or inept teaching? And, finally, do they work as well as reports indicate, or are we really just observing an imaginary effect?

Let me dispose of these objections one by one. The danger in the use of these particular medications (a term which I prefer to use instead of drugs) is no greater than with any other group of effective agents used in the treatment of any other physical disorders. When prescribed and followed by a knowledgeable physician in the proper dosage, there is a remarkably safe margin between the effective treatment level and the level of true toxicity. Children, even at an early age, tolerate fairly large doses with ease. By adjusting the amounts used and keeping close contact with the parents, doctors have been able in most instances to avoid the undesirable side effects of lowering of the appetite and interference with sleep. I know of no reports in the medical literature of any really serious dangers, such as damage to the bone marrow or impairment of liver function, which have occurred with some of the antibiotics or other agents widely used. I have been impressed by the careful studies in this regard conducted by many clinical investigators.

What about addiction or habituation? Will these children become so used to taking pills that they will, as some have suggested, turn to drugs in later life as an escape from any unpleasant situation? Since so many warnings have appeared about drug addiction in adolescents, this is perhaps the one aspect of medication that most alarms the parents — and also the children — with whom I have dealt. Fortunately, I have been able to reassure them that, since the use of amphetamines was first reported by Charles Bradley back in 1937, there has *never* been a case described in the medical literature of children becoming addicted to drugs who have been given any of these related preparations for the treatment of the condition which we call MBD. Since these medications are primarily stimulants which act on the sub-brain and brain stem rather than on the thinking cortex of the brain, most of the children are unaware of any real beneficial change occurring after they take their medication. They are not sent on any trip into a land of fantasy or euphoria; actually they seem to be in better contact with reality, and many have told me they can think more clearly. Habit-forming drugs are those which an individual deliberately takes to produce a desired effect, knowing ahead of time the results he anticipates. No such results are obtained with these medications. And as the children grow older, two deterrents to addiction appear. One, the physiological changes of adolescence often decrease the hyperactive behavior naturally. Two, the child usually develops a resentment to the whole idea of having to take medication. The sensitivity mentioned earlier which causes the child to object so much to being different may cause him to deliberately stop his medication, hiding his pills and reassuring his parents or teachers that he is still taking them. Such an attitude is hardly conducive to becoming a drug addict.

The next matter is such a tricky one that it is easy to become trapped in one's own argument. What are the *real* causes of learning difficulties? Aren't the schools overcrowded with bored children who receive little incentive from home to encourage them to succeed? Indeed many classrooms are, and it is difficult at first glance to decide which children truly have MBD and are proper candidates for medication. There is a real danger in having the pendulum swing too far, in suggesting that every child who misbehaves or does not perform well in school is learning-disabled. The astute and competent teacher will be able to note those specific characteristics of difficulty in the classroom which we have mentioned before as being so characteristic of the learning-disabled child — his peculiar spelling, his distorted handwriting, his inconsistency and variability, his disorganization — all of which should alert her to this possibility and suggest to her the advisability of having the parents seek a more intensive evaluation.

Do the medications really work? How can we be certain that the results are not due to the power of suggestion — what is called the placebo effect? When I first began to receive such glowing reports from parents of spectacular changes in their children after they began to take medication, I couldn't believe what I was hearing, and I also wondered about the validity of their statements. A pathologist friend of mine, who chided me earlier for gauging medical response on classroom improvement, also suggested that perhaps I was allowing my enthusiasm to rub off on my patients and their parents; convincing them that I had some sort of magic bullet I was certain would work, that I wanted to work and that the parents and teachers also wanted to work. Since everyone wanted so much for this miracle to happen, it did! I feel that I can refute this because I insisted that the parents *not* tell the teacher — or anyone — that the child was taking medication, and that they check with the teacher in a week or ten days and then report back to me. In the greater majority of instances, the teachers called the parents *before* this time, telling them how pleased they were that the child was not only behaving much better in the classroom but that his actual academic performance was improving.

One of the more disturbing objections to the use of medications (obviously made by workers who have never dealt with these children) is the suggestion that by administering these agents we are interfering with the "constitutional rights" of the individual child to learn how to develop self-control of his own accord. To any parent or teacher who has carefully observed a child with MBD trying to pay attention and follow directions, tormented and at the mercy of the overflow of distracting stimulation to which he must respond, such an idea is completely without foundation. The child with MBD has an organic biochemical disorder and needs medication to correct this imbalance; to suggest he can do this by will power alone would be equivalent to demanding that a diabetic child force himself to stop spilling sugar in his urine.

A most important effect of the medication, strikingly absent from the frightening reports in the lay literature which have overstressed the behavior-modifying aspects of these medications, is the improvement in the child's classroom achievement, which usually causes the teacher to comment on how much better the child is able to handle his school work. Because of the unfortunate publicity and the association with calming medications given to adults, many non-medical observers have thought the children were being placed on tranquilizers. Most of the medications used for slowing down adults do indeed slow the child down, but they also dull his intellectual processes and learning capacities as well. The medications used to help the MBD child — dextroamphetamine, methylphenidate, imipramine and nortriptylene — are stimulants. They do produce what appears to be a calming effect upon the child, but they do so by stimulating those centers in the sub-brain and brain stem which have to do with filtering out irrelevant impulses. They thereby allow the child to improve his attention span and concentration (see Chapter 3). Whether or not these medications actually stimulate the cortex or thinking areas of the brain is still a matter of controversy, but there is no doubt that most of the MBD children who take them begin to perform better in cognitive tasks. I always explain to parents that the medications are not going to raise their child's intelligence level one iota, but will allow him to utilize what learning capacities he does have much better.

By far the most important beneficial side-effect of medication is the improvement brought about in the child's own self-esteem. The value of such self-esteem can hardly be measured. Take, for example, a telephone call I received recently from a father who was reporting on his son's progress, as I had asked him to do. "Doctor," he said, "I just had to read you Bobby's report card — all B's and C's after nothing but D's and F's. I realize we still have a long way to go, but let me tell you about the nicest thing that has ever happened to us. Last night Bobby's teacher called his mother and told her how pleased she was that the other children were so proud of the way Bobby had improved." The one thing MBD children want most desperately — acceptance by their fellows — was finally coming to this boy after the humiliation and frustration of not being able to keep up.

Lately I have been more interested in finding out just how the children feel about the medication and whether or not they themselves have observed any results. One mother called me to let me know how excited her daughter was because she told her mother that now she can skip rope backwards, and she knew those pills were making her do it! I told her mother to tell Sally that those pills were not making her do anything. They were just letting the real Sally come out at last, and the real Sally was the one who could skip rope. Another mother who brings her children to our state clinic told me her older child who was eleven, and who had been very hyperactive and inattentive in the classroom, had settled down so much that his teacher was able to report good progress. Her younger son, age nine, had not been actually hyperactive in the classroom but was argumentative and constantly getting into fights in the halls and on the school grounds. "He's much better now," she told me, "but last Friday he asked me if he had to take his medicine that day. I told him he surely did and wondered why he had asked. Do you know what he said? He told me that last Friday was field day at school. He wanted to be in the races, but he ran much better when he could get mad at himself, and since he

Dr. Learre
I am having truble in
school. I am figting
in school, and tattle
tailing on other people.
I am having truble
on my subijefts.
I am not having
fun like I did last
year. The children
pick on me and
call me names
like, baby cry
baby, stupid, domy
and other names
like that

Examples of handwriting showing the disorganization and spelling errors typical of learning-disabled children. The drawing is also characteristic of the immature body concept seen in MBD children.

The medisin you gave me
helped me think better
and not be as nervis
as I usualy am when I
take tests.

Me and my sister
are hipractive (Dad no spelling)
and when we don't fell like
sitting down we will shap
our pincel led and get up
to go sharpen it then we
will wod up a peice of paper
and go through it away

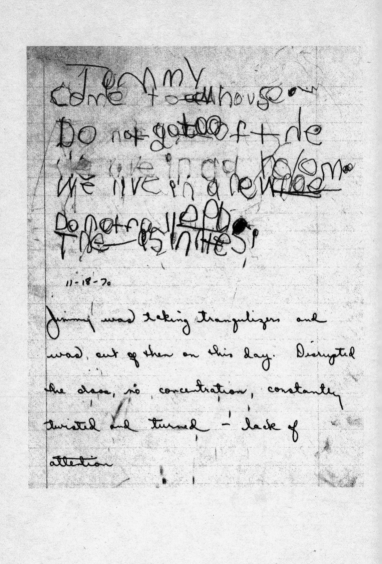

Jimmy
Come to d house
Do not get off the
we live in a new
Do not go out
the steps

11-18-70.

Jimmy was taking tranquilizers and
was out of them on this day. Disrupted
the class, no concentration, constantly
twisted and turned — lack of
attention

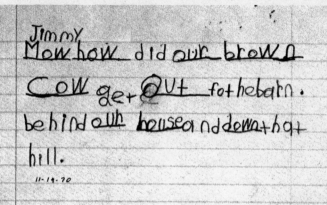

Jimmy

Mow how did our brown
cow get out fothebarn.
behind our houseanddownthat
hill.

11-19-70

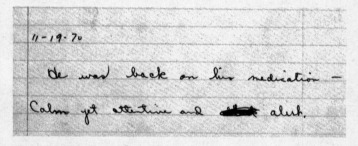

11-19-70

He was back on his medication —
Calm yet attentive and ~~alert~~ alert.

These two samples of the work of a nine-year-old boy show the beneficial effect of medication on his classroom performance. His teacher who thought he was taking tranquilizers suspected that he had missed his medication when his work deteriorated. She called this to his parents' attention. They resumed the medication, and the teacher noted the dramatic improvement in performance the next day.

has been taking the medicine, he doesn't get mad any more!" This was one time I had no objection to his skipping that day's medication, for Bruce won his race.

The effects on the child are duplicated by the effects on his parents. One mother told me how relieved she was, not because her child was behaving better and making higher grades, but because all the things that she had been blaming on herself had now been proven groundless. Another wrote to me of her observations concerning her eleven-year-old daughter: "Whatever [the medication] is, it's wonderful. Now our little girl is everything opposite; instead of light-headedness, it's light-heartedness; instead of having nervous frustrations, she is calm. . . . She said to me, 'Mother, thanks for always helping me.' Can you imagine how it made me feel? She knows the difference and she's so happy now."

In spite of these warm and glowing reports, I realize that we have not cured these children of their disorder. Most of them will continue to have good days and bad. They will grow and need their dosage adjusted or their medication changed, and they will probably still be somewhat disorganized or lack the ability to learn some specific subjects. Some will require medication for one year or less, while others may continue to need it through high school and on into college. But if we can turn the tide to help these children be recognized and accepted at school by their teachers and their classmates, if we can finally help build a bond of warmth and understanding between them and their parents, their future will be so much brighter. The gratifying results obtainable with medications make it mandatory that every classroom teacher understand MBD and be able to recognize those children who need further observation for the possibility of MBD, and also that every physician familiarize himself with the diagnostic tests and the therapeutic weapons at his command.

PART THREE

INTRODUCTION:
FORMING A TEAM

In the spring of 1969 I was invited to speak at the International Meeting of the Association for Children with Learning Disabilities on the subject of parent counselling. My good friend and colleague, Dr. Hyman Gardsbane, was national president-elect that year, so I asked him about the type of audience I might anticipate. The format would have to be different if I spoke to teachers about working with parents, if I talked directly to parents about handling their children, or if I discussed with other physicians my feeling concerning our role as parents' counselors. When he told me that I probably would have a mixture of all three, I realized that I had to come up with an approach that would be understandable to all, without being too complicated for the non-professionals or too trite for the more knowledgeable listeners. From this I developed the concept of the three R's of learning disability, *realization, recognition* and *remediation,* to explain how those who wanted to help an LD child could better understand him. Realization involves the acceptance of the fact that this condition actually exists, for there are still many who simply cannot believe that learning disability is a true entity. Recognition tells us how to identify the children who have this disorder and how to differentiate them from those who do not. And, most important of all, remediation gives us the means of actually helping the child to cope with his disability and better compete in the regular classroom. The session turned out to be a most interesting one, and from it came the idea that, if we are going to make real inroads into solving the learning disability problem, we will all have to join hands and work together as a team — teacher, parent and physician.

Many programs have been developed to improve the educational progress of the child with learning disorders. Each is enthusiastically endorsed by its developer and his or her followers. Since I am not an educator, the scope of their works will not be covered in detail. Rather I will attempt to suggest to the classroom teacher those measures which I have found most helpful on the basis of my personal experience. A list of references recommended for additional reading for each member of the learning disability team is furnished at the end of this book.

10.

THE LEARNING DISABILITY TEAM:
THE TEACHER

By virtue of her position as the front-line contact between the child and his parents and the whole educational system, the teacher finds her role as a member of the learning disability team a dominant one. The "trenches" are in the classroom, for here is where the child succeeds or fails, so the teacher is the only member of the group who is actually dealing with the crux of the problem every day. She is thrust into the midst of the action whether she likes it or not. She has the first opportunity to recognize the child's particular difficulty, and therefore must assume the obligation of informing the parents what is taking place and what can be done to help the child. She must act as the intermediary in obtaining the necessary evaluation and other diagnostic studies, depending upon the facilities available in her school system and her community. And out of necessity she may be the one called upon to arrange for the indicated remedial education, even to the point of performing these services herself. I don't know who should be considered captain of the learning disability team in all cases, but usually my vote must go to the teacher.

In working with teachers who deal with learning-disabled children, I have found that they can be classified into three main types. The first type is the teacher who refuses to accept the existence of learning disability. She believes that all this concern is really unnecessary and will prove to be a passing fancy, and is convinced that these children will some day all be shown to be either mentally retarded or emotionally disturbed. She thinks that meddlesome doctors should stick to practicing medicine, should stop trying to drug these children and leave their education to the educators. She is content to follow the firm curriculum that has been handed down to her, and is determined that all her pupils shall learn the facts that she dispenses as unassailable truths exactly the way she teaches them. Besides, she will often say, even if there are one or two children with learning problems, how can she devote special attention to them when she has thirty or thirty-five other children in her classroom?

The second type is the teacher who has heard a little about learning disability and who recognizes in the description of it some of the children in her classes who have puzzled her. She has spent time observing these children struggling with their studies, has talked to their parents about them, and somehow just can't accept the fact that they are all mentally deficient or that their difficulties come from poor parental handling. But she feels trapped by the system which insists that she test and grade all her children the same way, and that she fail the ones who have not attained a certain predetermined level of competency. She would like to spend more time with each individual child, but with all the extra things she has to do, such as collecting lunch money, helping in the various drives in her school, and preparing and grading tests and correcting all the homework that she must assign, she finds herself overwhelmed. She recognizes that some children need special help, and may refer the parents to a counselling agency or child guidance clinic, but seems unaware of what she can actually do in her own classroom.

The third type (may her tribe increase) is the teacher who understands the special nature of the learning-disabled child, and not only is interested in the disorder itself but also is determined to find out what she, as a classroom teacher, can do to help. She recognizes that children have unique differences in capabilities and skills, and tries to handle each child as individually as possible. She is not afraid to deviate from standard classroom routine, is willing to try innovations that she has heard about, or even invent some of her own, and is continually looking for ways to make the learning experience more interesting, not only for the learning-disabled child but also for all the children under her supervision. She is aware of the importance of success and is willing to bend a little in the matter of grading so as to minimize discouragement. When the occasion demands, she is willing to spend extra time after school with the child who is having trouble so that she can better observe his work away from the clamor and pressure of competition that is always present during regular school hours.

Most important of all, she is a warm human being, capable of appreciating the sensitive feelings of the learning-disabled child who is afraid of making a mistake and exposing his deficiencies to all his classmates. She knows how it feels to be embarrassed and laughed at, and is keen enough to anticipate these situations, thereby keeping the humiliation and frustration down to a bare minimum. She never uses sarcasm or ridicule, never criticizes the learning-disabled child in front of others, and never suggests that he could do better if he would just try harder. She knows how desperately the child really wants to learn and is prepared to help him as much as her situation will allow. Understanding the true nature of his problem, she does as the old song says, "accentuate the positive and eliminate the negative," praising him for his successful accomplishments and trying to find those things he does well rather than harping on his failings. She tries her utmost to make the child comfortable in the classroom, realizing the importance of release from tension and anxiety as a basic necessity for learning to take place. When she recognizes his distorted handwriting and confused spelling as a sign of his underlying disorganization, she will not send him to the blackboard to reveal his shortcomings for all to see. When she appreciates the child who has problems reading aloud in front of others, she will skillfully avoid calling upon him to subject him to this ordeal. If forced to test and grade the learning-disabled child along with the others in his class, she will understand that for him especially, *fail is a four-letter word*, and, while remaining fair and honest, she will let the child know she understands how much harder he has been trying. The notes she writes on his paper will indicate that she likes him or thinks he's a fine boy, instead of expressing disappointment or disgust. Peer pressure or methods of coercion, such as keeping him in after school, assigning extra homework, barring him from extra-curricular activities or sending him to the principal or parent for punishment, are not going to help the child with MBD learn any more readily.

In addition to her direct responsibility to the child, she recognizes the importance of the parents as members of the learning disability team and is capable of guiding them in the proper role. She is familiar with all the resources available in her area to evaluate the LD child and is prepared to take the initiative in securing services and interpreting the results to the concerned parents. She may be called upon to act as a go-between for the parents with the school authorities, giving them the benefit of her counsel concerning such important decisions as whether the child should attend a special class or have a special school placement. Through her contacts with other teachers and counselors, she may be able to help the parents find special tutors to help the child with individual subjects that are offering him particular difficulty.

The teacher is also prepared to act as a liaison with the third member of the learning disability team, the physician. Having observed the beneficial effects of medications on other children, and recognizing their limitations as well as their advantages, she contributes valuable information by her hour-by-hour and day-by-day observations of the child's improvement in attention span, and specific performance in the stress of regular classroom activity when it really counts. When medication is required during the school hours, she oversees its administration without unnecessarily embarrassing the child or exposing him to the curiosity of others. When adjustment of dosage is required, she can notify the parents to seek the physician's advice to make the necessary changes, advising the parents of the results she has noted, and encouraging them to continue as long as she finds it necessary and helpful. But enough of these generalities — let us examine what *specific* measures the teacher can take as a responsible member of the learning disability team.

Early Recognition

By now it should be obvious to all concerned that the earlier the learning-disabled child is diagnosed the greater is the likelihood that remedial and medical intervention will be successful. The kindergarten or first-grade teacher who is familiar with the characteristics of MBD will be able to detect a potential learning disability even before it becomes manifest in a fixed manner. Any child who seems immature, who cannot sit still, pay attention or follow instructions as well as others in the class, who is noticeably clumsy or awkward in handling himself, who cries more readily or seems more sensitive than the other children of his own group, should at least arouse the teacher's suspicion, and cause her to discuss with the parents the possibility that the child has learning difficulties. If the child has trouble in staying within boundaries when coloring with his crayons, or is clumsy in holding his pencil, the teacher should take notice, and observe whether or not these skills improve as the child becomes more familiar with his classroom tasks.

The inexperienced teacher may be unwilling to trust her own judgment merely on the basis of her observations in the classroom, especially since the manifestations of MBD are essentially those of delayed developmental maturity, as was discussed in Chapter 1. How can one be certain, for example, that a particular child has difficulty because of an organic biochemical problem, or because he simply has not had enough experiences with the tools of learning, or has been so overprotected that the classroom environment with a lot of other children is just too frightening for him? What are the specific attributes that a teacher should look for to allow her to predict, with some degree of assurance, that she has found a likely prospect for future school troubles? The best answers that I have found are presented in the work of Katrina de Hirsch and her co-workers who developed a battery of thirty-seven different tests which were given to a group of children at the kindergarten level. These same children were then re-evaluated at the end of the second grade for learning disorders, especially in reading. The observers found that ten specific tests gave a high rate of correlation and could be used with confidence to suggest what children were high risks for academic failure. Some, such as the Bender Visual Motor Gestalt and the Wepman Auditory Discrimination Tests, have been mentioned earlier. Others such as the Horst Reversals, Gates Word-Matching, Word Recognition I and II, and Word Reproduction and Categories can be found described in detail in their publication which is included in the suggested reading list. Two of the tests that require no scientific training at all, and can be used by any interested teacher, are the way the child uses a pencil and the number of words he uses to tell a story.

Teacher–Parent

Because the impact delivered by the person who first tells parents that something may be wrong with their child can be so devastating, the teacher who recognizes the child must be familiar with the nature of learning disability and must learn to individualize her approach as much as possible. She should be aware that what she says may not be nearly as important as how she says it. She must avoid such labels as "brain-damaged," "under-achiever," "slow learner," even "learning disability" until she has had time to meet the parents and discuss the child generally. She has to convince the parents first and foremost that she likes their child, that she is primarily interested in his welfare, and that she knows his good points as well as his failings. Unless the parents are handled cautiously and brought along gradually to fully comprehend their child's problems, they may resent the idea that their child is less than perfect and may take the teacher's well-meaning suggestions as pointing out their failings as parents. Since many of the children with learning disabilities give no indication of the impending trouble before they are confronted with the necessity of competing in the classroom, their parents may feel justified in blaming the school for all the trouble. As anyone who has a learning-disabled child will readily testify, the teacher who will listen sympathetically and avoid any suggestion of smugness or overbearing authority can do much to help parents through a time which is as difficult for them as for their child.

The teacher who detects the child with learning disability for the first time in the third or fourth grade will find her task in bringing the problem to the attention of the parents easier or more difficult, depending upon how her predecessors have acted. For the parents who are well aware that their child has been having difficulty with learning, the intervention of an understanding teacher can be a godsend, especially if they have been advised that their child will outgrow all of his problems, or that they are the result of their inefficiencies as parents. If their child has been badly handled, if he has been ridiculed or humiliated in front of his classmates, if they have been put through the "wringer" as Steve's mother was (and her story is by no means rare), they may have built up such a wall of resentment that the sincere, well-meaning teacher may find herself disappointed by their resentment and apparent lack of appreciation of her efforts. Only by a non-critical, honest, objective discussion of what she has observed in the classroom can the teacher bring parents around to the understanding and cooperation essential if the child is to receive help.

The teacher's role as a counselor does not stop with her association with the parents, for she will often find herself in the role of advisor to the evaluators and even to the school administrators with whom she must deal. The concept of learning disability is still not as widely accepted as it should be, and the knowledgeable teacher may find herself at odds with those who would still lean heavily on the idea that the environment is the cause of the child's problem. However, by giving her associates the benefit of her experiences, our third type of teacher may be able to win over some converts from the second type and even the first.

Remedial Education

How much the individual teacher can accomplish in the regular classroom situation will depend entirely upon the circumstances under which she must teach in her particular school. She is subject to the regulations imposed by the administrators and school board policies of her own community. If her classes are crowded and her time limited, she may find herself frustrated at every turn. If she is interested and is granted the freedom to do so, she may be able to perform enough diagnostic work on her own so that, even if unable to carry out any specific remedial techniques herself, she can work hand-in-hand with the tutor or research-center teacher, giving the benefit of her first-hand observations of the child's improvements or additional needs.

The best and most concise advice for classroom management that I have ever heard was presented by Empress Y. Zedler to a seminar on learning disabilities that we were privileged to hold in Shreveport under the auspices of the local Association for Children with Learning Disabilities and the Louisiana Easter Seal Society. This outstanding educator, truly a "teacher's teacher," urged those present to adhere to the following rules.

1. Try to transfer the child from auditory symbols to graphic written symbols at the kindergarten level.

2. Allow the child to use whatever props he needs — reading with his finger as a pointer, counting on his fingers and toes, and so forth.

3. Advise parents *not* to do their children's homework for them.

4. Let the child talk as he writes, giving him multi-sensory reinforcement.

5. Emphasize his *strengths* — find by which pathway he learns. Every child can do *some* reading.

6. Teach cursive writing, since it does not break the sequence of letters as printing does.

7. De-emphasize to the parents and the child the importance of grades, but let the child know how happy everyone is for the success that he attains.

Evaluation of the child's reading, writing and spelling difficulties by the Myklebust-Boder technique, previously referred to in Chapter 3, appears to offer a simplified method for the regular teacher who wishes to be in a position to advise more intelligently those who will be doing the remedial work with the child. Briefly, the evaluation can be carried out as follows. A list of twenty words based upon the frequency of appearance in books used from pre-primer up to senior high school level is used. (The seventh and eighth grade list, for example, includes such words as "recline," "charitable," "Susan," "trudge," "poorly," "fireman," "devoted.") The child is evaluated for word recognition, spelling and reading comprehension.

Word Recognition

Part 1. "Flash" — child looks at word for one second; if he can identify it correctly, he goes on to the next word; if not, he goes on to:

Part 2. "Untimed" — he is allowed to look at the word as long as he wishes, then try again.

Part 1 tests his actual sight vocabulary, Part 2 tests his word-association skills. Those words which he cannot read either way are called his "unknown" vocabulary.

Spelling Study

1. Eight words from the known vocabulary are given for the child to write (or to spell orally if he is unable to write).

2. Eight words from the unknown vocabulary are then given. The manner in which he handles the words from his sight vocabulary shows his ability to revisualize words, the ones from his unknown his ability to spell phonetically.

Reading Comprehension

The child is given a paragraph from his grade level or below to assess his reading comprehension and see whether or not his ability to read is improved when he uses words in a total context.

As noted before, the dyslexic child can then be assigned to one of three groups. The child in the first group is strong visually, so he will read well those whole words that he recognizes by sight, but when he encounters a new word, no matter how simple, he cannot sound out the elements and build them into a word. Even in the words he knows, he may not be able to identify the individual letters. He reads better in context, but if he finds an unfamiliar word, he will either skip it or substitute an entirely different sounding but applicable word, such as "mother" for "parent" or "airplane" for "train." His spellings are very distorted and he can correctly handle only those words which he can wholly recognize.

The child in the second group acts as if he were seeing each word for the first time, reading laboriously and handling well only those words in which he can recognize the sound. He may spell better than he reads, but the non-phonetic words that he encounters are written as they sound: "ocean" he writes "oshun," "listen" becomes "lison," "sauce" is "sos." He spells poorly, but not as bizarrely as the child in the first group.

The child in the third group is called the hard-core dsylexic child, for he is weak in both visual and hearing skills. He shows persistent spatial problems, reversing letters such as b and o, p and g. His spelling is even more bizarre than that of the children in the other groups, and the severity of his disorder gives him a defeated attitude in school early in the game.

The importance of these groupings lies in the selection of the method for individual remediation. A child in the first group can best be handled by whole-word technique, since phonics are his weakness. He will learn more quickly when his reading efforts are reinforced by tactile-kinesthetic clues, such as are used in tracing out letters while speaking them. Following this, his teacher should try to convert him from a non-phonetic to a phonetic speller. A child in the second group may also need to start with a tactile-kinesthetic approach until he has learned the letters of the alphabet visually, after which he will do better with a remedial phonic program. A child in the third group will need a combination of these methods, with continuing re-evaluation in order to find a method which will give him some type of success. Dr. Boder found that the majority of the children she observed were in the first group, causing her to feel their difficulties in auditory perception and sound discrimination were more important as causes of dyslexia than visuo-spatial perceptual disorders. A more complete reference to her work will be found in the suggested reading.

Although we do not have space to include all the various methods currently in vogue in remedial education, we will mention briefly those which the teacher is most likely to hear about. The Orton-Gillingham technique involves a multi-sensory approach (visual, auditory-kinesthetic — see Figure 5), having the child say the sounds while feeling and copying the letters by tracing over the teacher's model. Later he is drilled until he can perform these tasks without using the sensory assists. The Fernald method stresses the addition of tactile methods (VAKT) primarily by tracing. The Frostig techniques stress visual-perceptual training, the Gattegno and Bannatyne methods use color clues as added sensory references, and the Initial Teaching Alphabet, as mentioned before, tries to cope with the un-phonetic state of the English language by using an entirely different set of graphic symbols which are constant in their pronunciation. Each method has its enthusiastic supporters and its detractors, so that one is often inclined to feel that the personality of the worker may be equally as important as the particular technique involved. The imaginative teacher will try one form of remediation and be ready to shift to another if she feels a change is indicated. She may be unable to do any of these in the classroom setting and find that only by a one-to-one approach can the child really accomplish anything. Some of her more hyperactive children may be so distractable that they may need to be shut off completely from the others in a cubicle, a technique developed by William Cruickshank. The teacher may be increasingly confused as she explores the literature and finds such a large number of methods recommended. However, she should realize that with many children, the mere fact that someone is *doing something*, that someone at long last has been willing to stop punishing the child for his shortcomings as if they were all his fault and is now trying to help him, may be the biggest step of all. Volunteer workers with a minimum of real professional training have been able to accomplish a great deal of good in some programs, indicating that we need not sit back because of an apparent lack of highly trained personnel.

Teacher–Physician

The assistance that teachers can give the physician in working together to help learning-disabled children is invaluable. They can help him persuade parents to accept their child realistically. They can convince administrators of the reality of MBD, and, now that medication is becoming widely accepted, can do a tremendous job in educating others about the value of this method of treatment as they actually see it work. By observing the child who is receiving medication from hour to hour during the day they can assist the doctor in regulating the individual dosage required, and, by recognizing his sensitivity and desire to be treated as a regular member of the class, can keep his embarrassment over the medication down to a minimum. They can let the physician know when a child is not receiving his medication regularly and can help the child build up his self-esteem by responding warmly when he begins to improve in his classroom performance. Teachers can be of great help in convincing skeptical parents and even other physicians of the value of medication.

This is not the place to review the fact that the teaching profession has been poorly accepted and underpaid, however I cannot help but protest at the blame that has been placed upon the school system as being responsible for the entire learning disability problem. It disturbs me to read the testimony given at the Congressional Inquiry by a widely read educator and author who has been telling us how children learn and how they fail. His statement reads, in part:

Might not one of the causes be the fact that we take lively, curious, energetic children, eager to make contact with the world and to learn about it, stick them in barren classrooms with teachers who on the whole neither like nor respect nor understand nor trust them, restrict their freedom of speech and movement to a degree that would be judged excessive and inhuman even in a maximum security prison, and that their teachers themselves could not and would not tolerate? Then, when the children resist this brutalizing and stupefying treatment and retreat from it in anger, bewilderment, and terror, we say that they are sick with "complex and little-understood" disorders, and proceed to dose them with powerful drugs that are indeed complex and of whose long-run effects we know little or nothing, so that they may be more ready to do the asinine things the schools ask them to do.

These are harsh words which in the light of our current knowledge can only be considered the results of either misdirected emotionalism or appalling ignorance. Perhaps there are many things about our schools that could stand improvement, but when a child writes "bruther" for "brother," "21" instead of "12" or "was" for "saw," and when his handwriting wanders all over the page as does that of the child with MBD, I fail to see how anyone could accuse the teacher of causing this by her "brutalizing and stupefying treatment." Some educators seem to be totally unaware of the fact that the learning-disabled child is *biochemically different*, that, while he may react more violently to harsh treatment in the classroom, and may be less able to tolerate the sheer boredom that he encounters when he feels left out of the discussions that he cannot understand, his basic underlying difficulty is the disorder that we now call minimal brain dysfunction. I would be the first to agree that MBD is indeed "complex and little understood." However, open-minded observers have seen what amazing progress these children have made under proper treatment with medications. We are learning more every day about medication and we are discovering what a valuable adjunct this can be to any remedial program. The letters that I have received from teachers relating what they have observed have been most rewarding. The teacher who understands the medical nature of the problems that these children show in the classroom will make the major contribution in reaching the goal toward which all members of the learning disability team are striving — allowing the child to achieve his maximum educational potential.

11.

THE LEARNING DISABILITY TEAM: THE PARENTS

Parents also come in three categories that relate to their attitudes toward their child and their willingness to actively participate on the learning disability team. Those of the first type refuse to accept the possibility that anything could be wrong with their child, and resent bitterly anyone who suggests that their child is having trouble learning. They are certain that the teacher must be wrong, since their child always seemed bright and alert before he went to school. If he is actually behaving badly in the classroom, they are sure it must be the school's fault, since they have never seen him act that way at home. They feel that if the school personnel would just spend more time teaching him correctly and stop all the testing, everything would get better. Parents of the second type are willing to admit that their child is not doing so well in school, but feel that if his teacher were a stricter disciplinarian, he would learn to do better. They are ready and willing to punish the child for being lazy or not really trying hard enough, and will comply with the suggestion that they take away some of his privileges, as his teacher often recommends. They may even resort to physical beatings when the child still does no better. They refuse to seek remedial or medical help for the child, because they are certain that the teacher has it in for their child, or that she is really not interested in her work or capable of stimulating his desire to learn. They may go along with the testing and even begin to follow some of the remedial recommendations, but soon lose interest when rapid improvement does not follow.

Parents of the third type recognize honestly and realistically that their child is not achieving in school as well as he should be and are anxious to listen to anyone who seems genuinely interested in helping him. They seek advice concerning how they can better handle their child at home and how to find the type of educational assistance that he needs. They may balk at accepting all the responsibility for their child's difficulties, but they are willing to change their attitudes about the treatment of their child at home to comply with any reasonable suggestions. Also, they will eagerly follow the teacher's recommendations concerning steps to find the person or persons who can help remedy their child's specific learning disabilities. They have read with interest the increasing amount of information appearing in the popular magazines and newspapers about dyslexia and learning disabilities, and react with an open mind to the advice they receive. They willingly attend conferences with school authorities about their child, and actively participate with other parents in the formation of groups, such as the Association for Children with Learning Disabilities, in their community.

As more parents become aware of the existence of learning disabilities, their involvement as members of the learning disability team takes on added significance and changes their relationship to their child, to his teacher and the remainder of the educational establishment, to the physician, and to other parents. Their role will be even more crucial as our knowledge concerning the factors leading up to learning disability increases, for, as parents, they are in the key position to help in its early recognition and possible future prevention.

Parent–Child

Parental attitudes play a crucial role in the development of the personality of any child, but for the child with MBD and learning disability understanding is doubly vital. Every child needs the ABC's of a parent-child relationship which form the basis for good interpersonal dealings within the family structure. He needs to be *accepted*, to *belong*, and to be *cared for*. The child with MBD, being slow to develop maturity, being overly sensitive, and having an underlying personality disorganization based on his biochemical makeup, over-reacts to anything which appears unfavorable to him in his environment. Because he does not follow the same pattern as other children, because he acts so differently, parents find it difficult to accept him in the usual manner. The normal rules of misbehavior and punishment simply do not work with these children, and their aberrant behavior seems unaffected by any type of discipline the parent tries. The child is alert enough to recognize that his behavior creates dissension in the home, thus affecting his acceptance into the family group, but he continues to act as he does, having good days and bad, without apparent rhyme or reason. As with all other children the need to belong to the group is inherent in the MBD child, but the very nature of his disorder seems to drive away those people who mean the most to him. His attitude of "do it my way or not at all," his inability to compete whether in the classroom or, if he is clumsy, on the athletic field, his volatile temper and poor self-control all combine to make him obnoxious to his peer group at times. When he gravitates toward younger children, as he often does, they soon begin to abandon him as well. The craving for affection seems excessive in the MBD child, yet those around him find it difficult to tolerate all the things that he does and still feel any tenderness or fondness for him. He is aware of this only too well, and when he comes home from school bitterly complaining that nobody there really likes him, his apparent paranoia may be based more on fact than fiction.

How can parents handle such a situation? How can they accept a child to whom no rule of child-rearing that as parents they have been taught to believe valid seems to apply? How can they teach a child to accept responsibility if he remains so immature that they cannot trust him to handle simple tasks that even his younger brother or sister can do? They may be advised to give their child more experiences in which he can be successful, only to find each attempt causes more frustration and anger. All the reassuring platitudes that they hear only increase their own frustration until it almost approaches in intensity the dissatisfaction of their bewildered and unhappy child.

I wish I could be glib and send parents away with an assurance of success in dealing with their MBD child. Every child with MBD is different, as his parents are, and no one formula is going to work for all. However, there are a few basic principles that do seem to help most of these children, so they are worth at least a try. The first suggestion is to try to create an environment for the child in which he is comfortable at home, just as his teacher tries to do at school. Regularity is the keynote — up every morning at the same time, meal time at the same hours, to bed every night at the same time. What might appear to some to be monotonous seems to offer a certain degree of security to the MBD child. He finds that routine is reassuring, since, come what may during his disorganized day, certain things will remain stable and positive. Next, try to avoid those situations which have proven to be difficult and which usually end up in violent confrontation. I realize this sounds like appeasement, and probably is, but parents have found that these outbursts have no preventive value in helping the child avoid future problems. It is well to allow him to express his hostility ("Tell me why you don't like math") instead of asking for trouble ("Well, what went wrong at school today?"), and try to listen and accept his feelings for what they are. And when he must "blow his top" don't try to yell him down or tell him how wrong he is, but simply send him away to his room or some place where he can give vent to his hostility alone. The child is aware of his own lack of self-control, and parents have told me how their child will come to them after the storm has abated, not necessarily to beg forgiveness, but to reassure the parent of how much they love him or her, hoping for the same reassurance from the parent in return.

Another way in which parents can help their LD child cope with his problems is to try to minimize the number of decisions the child must make through the day. Situations that are filled with uncertainty seem to bother the MBD child, increasing his frustration and resentment. One father told me how he used to take his family out to dinner to a certain restaurant as a treat for his wife and children, but whenever the waiter presented the long and varied menu of which the establishment was so proud, his MBD child would struggle from page to page, unable to make up his mind, while the other members of the family urged him to hurry up and not keep them waiting. This father solved his problem eventually by only going to a one-item restaurant whenever the family ate out, so that everyone had fried chicken, pizza, or hamburgers.

The problem of avoiding decisions becomes most acute in the family situation where there are other children involved. Parents want to guide their children to become self-assured and confident as they advance toward maturity, but for the MBD child the contrast between his abilities and those of his siblings is a constant reminder that he is different, and it is almost impossible for the parents to sit down and explain why. How can you tactfully tell children that they have a brother who is "different?"

Fathers of MBD children occupy an especially warm spot in my heart, for I can understand what they must endure, particularly if their child is a clumsy, awkward boy. I grew up as a non-athletic boy, and I am sure I played right field more than any other boy in our neighborhood. (Some parents may not know this, but when the sandlot gang chooses up sides, the best athlete pitches, the next best catches, and the next few make up the infield. Since no one ever hits the ball out into right field, the last sad-sack to be chosen winds up there.) Physical ability frequently commands a higher degree of respect than classroom performance. The president of the senior class is more likely to be the football hero than the valedictorian. With the current enthusiasm for Little League baseball and team competition, the MBD child finds himself at a decided disadvantage. His mother may exhort his father to go out and play more sports with him and teach him how to hit and catch a ball better, but the father soon recognizes his son's lack of talent. The boy sees the disappointment in his father's attitude, and what should have been a rewarding time of coming closer together ends in disappointment for both of them.

The inability of the child with MBD to figure things out as readily as others because of his lack of development of abstract reasoning can also cause difficulty between parents and child. Sometimes these misconceptions can be amusing. In one instance a parent told me that his child thought the Country and Western tune, "Walking the Floor Over You," was about a man who had killed his wife and buried her in the basement of his house, so that he was actually walking the floor over her body! To treat the child with ridicule for failing to grasp subtle meanings is to drive him deeper into his shell. Nothing crushes his sensitive feelings more than to be laughed at. Parents should not take their child's understanding for granted, but should be willing to explain things more carefully — *away* from the other children in the family.

Now and then parents tell me that their biggest difficulty in securing family harmony, after starting their child on medical treatment, comes from grandparents or other relatives who rebel in horror at the very suggestion of medication for this difficulty. They intimate that anyone who suggests that a child's school problems might have a chemical basis must be losing contact with reality. I suggest that they remind these objectors of some other ideas which have seemed equally disturbing in the past. I can remember as an intern how every newborn baby in the nursery had to have a band of cloth, called a "belly-binder," around his abdomen as part of standard management, and no one would think of any variation. Then along came World War II, with shortages of metal for safety pins and fewer workers in the hospital laundries. When I came back from my four years in the service, I found that babies no longer left the hospital in belly-binders, in spite of the protests of many grandmothers, yet the babies all did just as well! In medicine we read of how bloodletting was formerly widely used for many ailments and not too long ago, surgeons talked about waiting for "laudable pus" to appear. More recently, I can remember how some infants with breathing difficulty were treated by irradiation of the thymus gland to cause it to shrink. Then it was discovered that the gland would shrink just as well without the X-ray treatment, and with much less hazard to the child.

When parents become aware that their child's learning disability is due to an innate lack of talent, like the lack of musical talent, their attitude changes from one of constant harassment and punishment to one of acceptance and understanding. Often the pendulum will swing too far, as the parents try to compensate for all the mistreatment dealt their child by showing pity, which the child does not need, or trying to do everything for him, which he needs even less. They try to handle all the child's homework for him and even buy special books and equipment so that they can undertake the remedial work themselves. But, as Dr. Zedler has so aptly noted, being a parent is an emotional task, and being a teacher is a technical one. No matter how well-meaning parents try to be, few possess the unshakeable patience required to handle all the repetitive work necessary in remedial teaching without allowing some of their exasperation to escape and become evident to their child. When parents complain of their inability to find a skilled tutor, I often suggest that they look for a competent teacher who understands their child's problem and will be willing to moonlight so that the child will have the benefit of individualized, one-to-one educational experiences. Some parents have obtained assistance by having a high school or college student act as a reader to their child, and many schools are beginning to develop actual remedial classes using older children, to whom younger children relate easily, to help the learning-disabled children in the lower grades. Often an older child or young adult who is not a member of the family makes an ideal instructor to teach the MBD child some physical activity of a non-competitive nature, such as swimming or bowling, which he can master to some degree. The teaching sessions are best handled alone, where no one else can watch the child and embarrass him.

Another factor related to their child's school performance which helps the parents understand his difficulties is the realization of the intensely competitive nature under which the child must attempt to learn. The constant emphasis on testing and grading, the ever present comparison with every other child, the certainty that every unsuccessful effort on his part will be permanently inscribed for all to see — all exert tremendous pressure on the already anxious and sensitive learning-disabled child. I have asked mothers how they would feel if every night they had to cook dinner standing at a stove surrounded by thirty other housewives, all standing at their stoves, knowing that every meal they produced would be graded and compared with everyone else's cooking. Competition may be the spice of life, but as adults we can avoid our individual inadequacies by taking up an occupation that does not readily reveal them. For the child in school, there is no such escape.

Parent–Teacher

The relationship of parent and teacher — these two important members of the learning disability team — is a sensitive one, for it requires a great deal of mutual understanding and respect to be successful in handling the learning-disabled child. The parent should be aware of the limitations and restrictions placed upon the teacher by the school system in which she must operate. Educators are, by their very nature, usually conservative, and the curriculum for any given semester is decided upon years in advance. Parents must realize that when we say fifteen or twenty percent of the children are learning-disabled, this means that eighty percent are not. Educators can take some degree of credit for being able to take a mixture of youngsters from all sorts of backgrounds and with varied capabilities and move as many as they do successfully up the scholastic ladder.

Once parents realize that the teacher is as anxious as they are for their child to succeed in school, a feeling of mutual respect develops as they explore the steps necessary to help the child begin to achieve academically. Together, they can come to realize that the child, like all children, has specific talents as well as specific inabilities. If one of the skills that the child lacks happens to be in reading, writing or spelling, they will be aware that special measures are indicated, since these subjects are so important in classroom performance. The teacher may be willing to allow the child to bring a tape recorder to school, if he learns better by the auditory means, or even permit him to make recordings of his homework if he has unusual difficulty in expressing himself graphically. If she can do so, she may allow him to take his tests orally, and those examinations for which he must write she will grade accordingly. The entire matter of grades and report cards should be clarified since so much stress has been given to competitive comparison. Dr. Zedler suggested to us that report cards should be used only as a guide for one educator to assist another educator in helping a child, and not as a means of punishment or coercion to force any child to do better. She advised the parents present for her talk at the conference on learning disability to "turn those cards over, ask where to sign your names, do so, give your child a big hug and don't ever look on the inside!" But the children themselves are aware of the fact that grades are considered the major criteria by which their accomplishments in school are judged. Many a child does not really have a true "learning" disability, for he is learning all the time, but he cannot put down on paper under the stressful conditions of an examination what knowledge he possesses. He is therefore doomed to failure until the educators become aware of the discrepancy between his knowledge and his ability to express it, and are willing to adjust accordingly. Together parent and teacher can do much to guide the child around these obstructions to his educational progress and help him attain some level of achievement.

Parent–Physician

The relationship between the parents and their child's physician working together on the learning disability team can be a rewarding experience for both. The parents can bring to the physician an accurate and informative record of their child's developmental progress and current attitudes, an invaluable tool in assisting the physician in making his diagnosis, since often there is little to be discovered by the usual methods of medical examination. When the physician prescribes medication, the parents must keep him informed of the progress and changes seen in their child's activities and behavior and help the physician adjust the proper level of medication for maximum benefit. They should bring the child back for re-evaluation if necessary. Also, they should act as a liaison between the educators and the doctor by reporting to him the teacher's evaluations of the child's progress. Often the arrangement works in a reverse fashion, for in many instances, it is the parent who brings the material about her child's condition to the teacher, who may not yet be aware of the medical nature of this disorder. And when the medication does produce the desired and often unbelievable improvement in the child's behavior and classroom performance, his parents are the ones who begin to spread the good news, encouraging other parents to seek proper medical advice and attention for their LD children. Nothing can be more heartening to a physician than to have parents bring a child to him with the comment that, after observing their neighbor's child and his response to medication, they have finally reached an appreciation of their own child's problem after misunderstanding him for such a long time. When a parent writes, "Thank you for giving our child back to us," it would be a cold physician indeed who did not feel deeply moved.

Parent–Parent

The impact that knowledgeable parents can have on other parents of children suspected of having learning disability has not been emphasized sufficiently, and I have found them invaluable in spreading our present knowledge about the problem. Such organizations as the Association for Children with Learning Disabilities (ACLD) hold great promise for helping the future status of children with MBD and learning disabilities, for the strength of the combined efforts of these concerned parents and other interested individuals is being felt in various state legislatures and even on a national level. Insistence upon a more equitable educational system for these children is bound to bring results. All of the effective established movements for children with handicaps

— such as mental retardation, cerebral palsy, muscular dystrophy, and others — were started not by physicians, educators, or other professionals, but by parents. With the current philosophy for bettering the welfare of all minority groups, certainly the twenty percent who make up a real "oppressed minority," considering the way so many have been mistreated in school, should receive the attention and understanding they deserve.

Another aspect of the problem with which parents' groups can contend is the matter of the validity of having insurance payments cover the additional expenses involved in obtaining the not inexpensive special education for the learning-disabled child. Since neither dyslexia nor any other learning disability is officially listed as a disease in the actuary offices, it will require an increase in general knowledge about these conditions to effect the necessary changes, and the educational program of the ACLD seems to have made an excellent beginning in this direction. Other national and state organizations, notably the Easter Seal Society, have demonstrated their interest in learning disabilities, and through the diversity of their facilities, promise even greater advances in helping these children and their parents in the days and years ahead.

12.

THE LEARNING DISABILITY TEAM: THE PHYSICIAN

Even physicians come in three varieties in regard to their feelings about the role they should assume on the learning disability team. Those in the first group are too busy treating sick children to be concerned with such conditions as behavior disturbances or school problems, which they feel more properly belong in the realm of the psychologist or psychiatrist. "Leave the education to the educators" is their advice as they follow the suggestions of any or all of the blind leaders whom we discussed in Part II. Having dealt with so many overly concerned mothers through their years of practice, they know that many of the imaginary ailments about which anxious parents complain disappear through natural development, so they usually are strong adherents to the "let 'em outgrow it" philosophy.

The physicians who comprise the second group are also very busy doctors, but they sense that there must be something significant behind the growing number of articles now appearing in the medical literature concerning learning disabilities and MBD. As they listen to the conflicting opinions and note the controversies over diagnostic tools such as the EEG and the use of behavior-modifying medications, they feel that they lack the necessary specialized training in neurology or psychiatry to handle these children properly. While willing to carefully examine these children, they become discouraged when they are unable to discover anything of significance by their usual methods of physical diagnosis or laboratory study, so they look around for someone else to whom they can refer the child for a more comprehensive evaluation. Through all the recent controversy about "drugs in the classroom" they have been aware of the fact that stimulant medications are being used with considerable success, but they feel their experience is too limited to justify taking such a step. In addition they are just unable to find the time necessary in already crowded office schedules to satisfactorily deal with these children and their parents.

The physician in the third group has become aware of the magnitude of the problem of learning disability and is willing to concede that any disorder comprising nearly one fifth of his entire practice demands that he become vitally concerned about what he can do to help. He recognizes that any physician who cares for children must become more concerned with what takes place in school, just as the industrial physician must be aware of the hazards to his patients in the factories in which they work. Schools represent the factories in which our children labor, spending a good part of their waking hours in this highly competitive environment. He realizes that the parents who bring their children to him for advice are sincere in their desire to obtain help, so that he is willing to actively intervene and assume the responsibility consistent with his proper position on the learning disability team.

Physician–Parent

Since the physician's contact with the learning-disabled
child is largely through the child's parents, much of the
effectiveness of his treatment will depend upon the manner in which he explains the nature of their child's disorder to them, and develops the necessary rapport with
them to secure their whole-hearted cooperation with his
method of treatment. The physician will vary in his approach depending upon his own personal experiences and
the methods he has found to be most successful. He recognizes the importance of a child's academic success to
parents and understands how the behavior indicative of
MBD can be interpreted by parents as evidence of the
inadequacies of their concepts of child-rearing. He may
note that parents may need a great deal more supportive
care than he feels able to give, and may wish to refer
them to a colleague whom he has found capable and
sympathetic in handling such problems. Through working with a number of children having learning disabilities,
he becomes familiar with the schooling situation, both
public and private, in his own community, and is able to
discuss the most satisfactory placement for each child
with members of the educational field. He is aware of the
existence of those who would exploit the child for their
own financial gain and is prepared to help the parent
avoid such traps, no matter how attractively they might
present themselves. His approach is a positive one, not
merely condemning those who do not agree with his position, but being willing to accept in good faith anyone
who will help the child. He can mobilize all the talent

available in his particular area and knows where to refer his patient for further responsible evaluation while steering clear of unproven methods which are unethically promoted.

Each physician develops his own technique in explaining to parents just exactly what he feels is wrong with the learning-disabled child. My personal preference, as stated earlier, is to point out the resemblance to deficiencies in musical skills or talents, which most parents will accept without question. Lack of musical talent has absolutely nothing to do with a person's IQ, motivation, malnutrition, how he was potty-trained, or any other environmental influence (although training and practice certainly can improve musical skill), and no stigma is attached to this lack of ability. We would certainly not tell a child that if he went home and practiced enough, if he *really* wanted to badly enough, he could sing just like Robert Merrill or Dean Martin or whoever his favorite might be. We would not punish him, or ridicule him, or make fun of his lack of talent in front of others, or take away his bicycle or television privileges until he learned to sing more melodiously. And if he showed no interest in music we would not accuse him of being lazy. Has anyone *ever* seen a lazy six- or seven-year-old child? Is it possible that learning disabilities represent a lack of talent in the communication skills and that the child who cannot understand arithmetic is tone-deaf for math? This lack of specific skill and talent is becoming more evident as we uncover more of the learning problems that these youngsters show. I recently saw a young man, in his junior year in college, who had been forced to change his major from music to sociology, because in order to get his degree in music he would have to learn to play the piano, and, as he told me, he just couldn't make his hands do what he wanted them to. In investigating further, I read a report from a physician in Boston who had as a patient a young woman who had graduated in elementary education and wished to teach the primary grades in her hometown. However, in order to do so she needed to learn to play the piano so she could have her little charges march back and forth and teach them to sing "My Country 'Tis of Thee." This young woman spent two years of her time and money and still couldn't learn to play the piano. She finally solved her problem by obtaining her license in a neighboring state and then obtaining reciprocity! The better we understand individual variations in skills, interests, and capabilities, the better we will understand the complexities of learning disability.

Physician–Teacher

When the physician first becomes involved with the educational profession in the matter of learning disabilities, he may feel as if he has ventured into a strange new world with an entirely different set of ideas and a language with a jargon all its own. Instead of discussing blood counts and immunizations, he now finds himself involved with ITPA's and WISC's, and instead of interpreting X-rays and electrocardiograms, he now must study Bender-Gestalt drawings and samples of handwriting and spelling. In place of discussing the fever chart of his patient with the hospital nurse to decide the course of treatment, he now must question the teacher as to whether or not his patient is doing fine during the morning hours but demonstrating less self-control and concentration in the afternoon, as an indication of how well the medication is working. If he encounters the type of teacher who refuses to co-operate, he may remember the story of the sign in the hamburger stand which read "We have an arrangement with the bank — they don't sell any hamburgers and we don't cash any checks!" and he may be tempted to stay out of the scene entirely. But once the teachers begin to note how the child improves in the classroom and the tutor or remedial educator reports how much more amenable the child appears to her corrective techniques, the physician will be accepted as a full-fledged member of the team. He can make a valuable contribution to the entire learning disability program by accepting invitations to speak to PTA groups and in-training workshops, for most teachers are avidly interested in learning disorders, recognizing that their previous educational training has often been lacking in this area.

All of us realize more each day what an important part school experiences play in the development of every child's personality. Freudian disciples may consider this utter blasphemy, but I really believe that what happens to a child in school may be as important, or more important, to his emotional well-being and development than what happens to him at home. The child needs parents who love him (and it is tragic to find a child whose parents do not), but I don't believe the child himself feels any sense of accomplishment if they do. "They have to," he thinks, "I live with them and belong to them!" But at school, things are different — teachers don't have to love him, and the children at school do not have to accept him. Here is his first real chance to prove his own worth as an individual, and if he fails, the damage to his self-esteem and inner security is irreparable. When he finds his learning problems cause his teacher and parents to be disappointed in him, when they continually suggest that his difficulties are caused because he is not trying, while he is doing everything he knows how to figure out what school is all about — well, I've already said it — this is the real cause of the emotional problems shown by nearly every learning-disabled child.

Physician–Child

The extent to which the physician becomes directly involved with the child during the course of remedial treatment will depend upon his own personal convictions. Some feel that it is better to sit down and discuss the matter openly with the patient himself, explaining the purpose of the medication, the rationale for its use, and the overall concept of learning disability to the victim himself. Others have found that the matter is rather touchy and that any specific reference to something being actually wrong with the child can have a harmful effect in jarring his already shaky morale and low self-esteem. No matter how carefully the physician phrases his findings, if the child suspects that the reason for all the concern is that there is something wrong with his brain — and he may have some definite suspicions along this line — the effect can be disastrous. For in the common vernacular, if anyone has something wrong with his brain, he must be either retarded or crazy. I had one young fellow just nine years old who glared at me across my desk and asked me if I were a psychiatrist. When I reassured him to the contrary he mumbled something under his breath about "not wanting to come see any 'shrink'!" The stigma attached to mental illness is well recognized even at these early age levels, adding to the concern that the child feels when everything seems to be going wrong at school and at home.

The problem of what to tell the child when he is placed on medication is another aspect of treatment that brings varied responses from concerned physicians. I am aware that most older children have been taught, as they should be, about the dangers of drug addiction, making them skeptical or even hostile to the idea of having to take any medication for a long period of time. I usually tell them, as I do the younger children, that I am giving their parents a little tablet that I want them to take, and that it acts "like a vitamin does." This is not lying to the child, since the medication does seem to work through the enzyme systems of the body; and I stress that I hope it makes them feel better just as vitamins do. Most of the children accept this very well, although after a while the older ones demand a better explanation. To them I relate their problem to that of a diabetic child who needs insulin daily to make up for his metabolic deficiency or to a thyroid-deficient individual who needs additional medication to bring his hormone level up to par. I have been particularly concerned about those youngsters who need medication throughout the day and have to take a tablet at noon to carry them through the afternoon school hours. One of my ten-year-old patients allayed my fears when his mother reported that he told his teacher, "I have to take this, 'cause I have a biochemical imbalance!"

How long each child needs to take the medication is another matter of concern both to him and his parents. My advice is that the child take it as long as he needs to, and as long as he thinks more clearly and improves in self-control. If he continues to improve in his academic performance, there is no harm in his taking medication even through high school and on to college. If and when the child finds he no longer requires the help that the medication has been giving him, he can stop without any harmful effects or signs of withdrawal. Some parents have tried discontinuing the medication during the summer months, then starting again when school opens in the fall. Others find that, once the child adjusts to the routine of daily medication, he feels better if he continues it year-round, since vacation time may be more irregular and confused, while school, although academically stressful, at least is regular and organized.

No matter what method is chosen, the fact still remains that the child himself is usually ashamed to talk about his problem. When I approach a new patient and ask him what he is doing in my office, he will usually point to his parents and say, "Ask them." Very few of the youngsters under my care have looked me in the eye and said they have problems learning in school, but I suspect most of them know why they have come, and they know that *I* know they realize why they are there. Tact and diplomacy must take precedence over all else during that first visit to instill confidence in the learning-disabled child that we are on his side.

Physician–Physician

The physician who adopts the third type of attitude described at the start of this chapter, soon finds himself anxious to convert his colleagues of the first and second type in order to aid the large number of children who need help. He may receive responses which vary from outspoken skepticism to downright hostility, and he soon recognizes that only time and continuing success in treating the learning-disabled child can bring about any widespread appreciation of the magnitude of the problem. Some of the most enthusiastic "believers" are physicians whose own children have been discovered to have learning disabilities and who have improved with suitable medication and remedial education.

Physicians have a three-fold obligation because of their unique position on the learning disability team. As mentioned before, the physician is an authority, so that when he speaks to a parent or an educational group he carries with him all the prestige of his profession. He has an obligation therefore to remain abreast of current knowledge, and advances in it, so that he may keep his allies from other fields informed. By so doing he fulfills his role as a doctor, since the Latin word *"docere"* means "to teach." Next he must act as a counselor, helping parents and educators alike avoid the mistakes so frequently made by the ill-informed. By his guidance he can help advise against failing a child and making him repeat a year in school, since the effect on the child's developing personality may be irreversible. He can make recommendations and suggest ideas concerning special classes and special schools. If he remembers how desperately the MBD child hopes to be treated like every other student and not to be designated as someone different or special, he will try to see to it that the child continues to be kept with his class if at all possible. He can encourage the school system to develop more sources to effect the individualized remedial help found most effective in educating the majority of learning-disabled children. Finally, he is a physician. He alone has the opportunity to follow the child's progress from the nursery through infancy and early childhood until he is old enough to enter school. He can determine from his association with the family if they are denying the child the experiences and opportunities for proper maturation by either overprotection or rejection. As the family physician, he can observe other members of the household and have a much more realistic appraisal of the child's overall background. Most important of all, he alone has the authority and power to write a prescription for medication to help the child, based upon his own clinical experience and observations. He recognizes his medical creed of *"primum non nocere"* ("First, do no harm") so that, by following established professional practice, he will not risk harming his young patient. This is how he would want his own child treated.

Each physician develops his own methods of medical treatment and follows those which he has found most successful. Among the medications now available I have found methylphenidate most flexible and adaptable, but of short duration, so that repeated dosage is required. I usually recommend giving the child his medication when he arises and when he comes home from school, avoiding medication after 4 P.M. If he has difficulty in the afternoon, I prescribe an additional dose with lunch, asking the teacher to make the procedure as inconspicuous as possible. Recently I have been favoring imipramine. It can be given as a single dose one hour before bedtime and often lasts throughout the next day; if necessary, the child can receive another dose on arising. I have almost completely stopped using the amphetamines because of their unfavorable publicity, and will occasionally try nortriptylene when the others do not bring the desired response. Each child needs to have his dosage individually adjusted, and quite often combinations need to be tried before success is attained.

Just as there are individual methods of medical management, diagnostic routines will vary according to the physician. No one test is absolutely indicative of MBD, but I have found the following method of examination to be helpful.

1. A thorough medical history and physical examination, with stress on the happenings during the prenatal period and birth process which might be important, should be taken. Vision and hearing should be carefully checked, although by the time most learning-disabled children reach my office these functions have been well studied. A history of colic, of frequent formula changes

due to what is often thought to be a food allergy, of extreme fussiness or excessive sleepiness during the first six months of life may be significant. Acquisition of certain levels of skill such as sitting, standing and walking alone should be inquired about. Sleep habits and development of night-time bladder control may give important clues, as does any deviation from normal speech development. The degree of hyperactivity, gross and fine motor coordination, and emotional stability also are pertinent.

2. A careful history of the school experiences of siblings, parents and grandparents should be taken if possible. The frequency (over 80 percent) of the familial incidence of learning problems has been noted, and careful tactful questioning may be required.

3. Developmental examination as a screen for MBD:

   a. Extra-ocular movements — observe how eyes function in unison following a penlight or other moving object.

   b. Laterality and body awareness (ask when the child is lying supine)

      (1) Are you right-handed or left-handed? Show me your right hand. When someone tells you to go to your left, how do you know which way to turn?

      (2) Put your right heel on your left knee; slide your foot down the front of your leg. Put your left heel on your right knee, and so forth. (Observe *how* the child does this.)

      (3) (Toe identification) I am going to move your toes up and down, and I want you to

tell me which toe I am touching and which way I have moved it. This is the big toe on your right foot, the one next to your big toe, the middle one, the one next to your little toe, the little one. This way, toward your head is up, this way is down. Now with your eyes closed, tell me which toe I am pushing and which way it is going.

(4) (Ask with the child sitting up) Put your right hand on your right ear; put your left hand on your left ear; put your left hand on your right ear; put your right hand on *my* right ear.

c. Gross and fine motor coordination (ask when the child is standing)

(1) Hop across the room back and forth on your right foot; now your left foot — which one hops better?

(2) I will bounce this tennis ball to you; bounce it back to me (observe preferred hand); now kick it back to me (observe preferred foot); look through this magnifying glass at your finger, holding it close to one eye so you can see your fingerprint (I use my otoscope to detect the preferred eye). Let me see you close one eye at a time. (Many children cannot close one eye and keep the other open at the same time — a frequent finding in MBD, indicating immature fine motor co-ordination.)

  d. Now draw me a picture of a boy, a tree and a
     house, then write me a note so I can learn more
     about what kind of boy you are.

This is not really a neurological examination, for teachers or nurses could do the same tests in a matter of ten
minutes. If the child shows marked right-left confusion
and poor toe identification, one can suspect some disorganization of coordinated nervous system function. His
drawings and especially his handwriting are the most
representative of his real classroom performance. The
marked discrepancy between what a boy can tell me and
what he can write for me is highly indicative of a lack of
graphic communicating skill. While unable to prove any
true diagnostic significance to this screening, I do feel it
suggestive enough to indicate a trial of medication. The
response that the child makes to medication, lengthening
of attention span, reduction of distractibility, improvement of emotional control, and better concentration, I
consider the most important evidence of the fact that he
does indeed have an inherent biochemical disorder.
When we receive reports of all those favorable effects, I
feel that our diagnostic suspicion of MBD has been confirmed, and we can expect some degree of improvement
in classroom performance. If we can maintain the child
in his regular classroom and find the necessary assistance
to learning on an individualized, one-to-one basis according to his specific needs, then our goal will have been attained and the purpose of our learning disability team
achieved.

EPILOGUE:
THE SAGA OF STEVE (Continued)

Steve has been on medication for nearly a week, so I know I soon will be receiving reports from his parents and teachers about his response to the treatment and his progress in the classroom. I wish it were always possible to give a glowing, optimistic prognosis and be able to state without a doubt he would soon begin to achieve academically and adapt socially, thus overcoming the two main obstacles in his young life. But each child is such an individual, and the differences we encounter so variable and inconsistent, that the treatment of the learning-disabled child is a precarious and often maddening undertaking. What has been the effect on his personality of the years during which he was humiliated and ridiculed by his teachers and classmates? Does he feel convinced by all the testing and evaluating to which he had been subjected that there is something desperately and irreparably wrong with him? Have his experiences so beaten him down that he is accustomed to failure and feels trapped in a hopeless situation from which the only escape is either retreating into a shell of total unconcern or striking back with hostility at a world which has treated him so shabbily?

And what of his parents — have they given up on Steve? Is it too late to convince them of the biochemical basis of his difficulties after all they have heard concerning his problems and how they have contributed to them? Have they been able to maintain any form of stability in their family life during all their trials? Can they still accept Steve for what he really is and not abandon him in despair as he approaches his crucial adolescent years?

Steve's future hangs in the balance and depends upon two things: the response that he shows to medication, and the adaptability of his environment in school and at home. If his medication begins to lengthen his attention span and help him improve his ability to organize his learning efforts, and if his teachers are knowledgeable and understanding with a sincere desire to help him, most of the battle will be won. By not informing his teachers that he was being started on medication we can be reasonably assured that their observations will be objectively accurate, so that when we take them into our confidence their attitude toward Steve will be as favorable as possible. Once he begins to achieve success instead of failure, recognition instead of ridicule, and acceptance instead of rejection, the vicious circle will be reversed and the outlook will be much brighter. When his teachers begin to find the things that Steve can do best, and give him a chance to demonstrate his abilities for all to see, the results can be most gratifying — you remember what was said about feedback.

With success at school will come success at home. The personality quirks and behavior problems associated with the LD child are annoying and difficult to live with, but the failure to achieve in school is the most pressing problem to Steve's parents, as it has been to most of the parents with whom I have worked. Once he begins to achieve in the classroom, and they can finally assure themselves that the problem has not been due to willful disobedience on his part or their ineptness as parents, most of their difficulties will be relieved. I am aware of reports from authorities who tell of parents who have used their child's learning disabilities as a crutch for their own emotional difficulties, who actually do not want their child to improve because helping him with his disorder has become their only source of fulfillment as a parent, but I feel these must be extreme cases and are rather rare. Parents have feelings and aspirations for their children, and some of their reactions to their own and their child's psychological mismanagement are quite understandable.

As we have noted all along, Steve does not have an illness which can be cured medically. Even though his response under medication in the classroom and at home may be dramatic, he will still require continued attention for his specific educational needs. Just how much his teachers can actually do in the classroom will depend upon the attitude at his school and the flexibility permitted in handling each individual child. Further evaluation may be required as a matter of educational protocol, and, while re-assessment is certainly desirable from time to time to appraise a child's progress or change under medication, there is no point in subjecting the child to useless repetitive studies unless something can actually be done to use the information obtained to help the child. There is little value in advising parents that their child needs special tutoring unless tutors are readily available, or that special classes would be the answer, if the school system offers none. Can you imagine the frustration felt by parents who are finally told what is actually wrong with their child and what should be done, but find that there is really no place for them to turn to for the assistance they need?

Steve's overall prognosis will be further affected by his age, since adolescence will produce added changes in his physical and chemical makeup that will alter his behavior and emotional control. All teen-agers have internal conflicts as well as difficulties in getting along with their parents and others about them, and the learning-disabled child is certainly no exception. Adjustments in the amount of his medication will be required, and continuing attention must be given to his individual social difficulties. If his low self-esteem and lack of self-confidence persist, he will fall behind in making contacts and relationships with girls, and may reach early adult life still an insecure and very immature individual. He will find that most teen-age girls look up to a confident, self-assured male companion, a role which he finds difficult to fill. Even if he can solve or at least compensate for most of his learning difficulties, he may find his emotional insecurity continues to plague him as a young adult. Further, his lack of capability or experience with abstract reasoning processes holds back his progress in career achievement.

The outlook is not altogether gloomy, for history is replete with instances of individuals who had childhood experiences strongly suggesting the presence of learning disability, yet who went on to outstanding success as adults. In their book, *Cradles of Eminence*, Victor and

Mildred Goertzel tell us that Woodrow Wilson did not learn his letters until he was nine or learn to read until he was eleven. Concerned relatives wrote his parents expressing their sorrow that he was dull and backward, yet this man became not only an outstanding educator as president of Princeton, but also one of our outstanding statesmen as the twenty-eighth President of our country. General George Patton was sent to boarding school at twelve to be specially tutored for West Point, because he could not read print even though he could write script. Thomas Edison is quoted as saying "I was never able to get along in school. I was always at the foot of the class . . . my father thought I was stupid," yet his inventive genius has never been duplicated. The brilliant neurosurgeon Harvey Cushing, whose explosive manners in the operating room were equalled only by his remarkable technical skill, was a poor speller even as an adult, writing "priviledge," "amatures," and "definate" in his correspondence. Eleanor Roosevelt is reported to have been poor in spelling, arithmetic and grammar, and was shy and awkward as a child and young woman. Even the great Albert Einstein was thought to be mentally dull by his teachers who found he had great difficulty in learning languages and was slow and hesitant in his speech. They reported to his parents that he seemed "adrift forever in his foolish dreams." To these dignitaries I can add a number of adults, perhaps less well known, but equally important to their families, who grew up to become physicians, ministers, architects, lawyers, craftsmen, merchants, or homemakers and whose children with learning disability are now patients of mine.

THE FUTURE FOR THE
LEARNING-DISABLED CHILD

What does the future hold for the learning-disabled child and what can we as members of the learning disability team do to improve his outlook? Beyond doubt, the most important contribution that we can make is to help remove the stigma now attached to this disorder by educating all those who deal with these children to recognize the problem for what it is, a structural neurochemical disorder, and to break away from the superstition and ignorance that has surrounded them for so long. With the information we now have, we can readily detect the learning-disabled child in kindergarten or the first grade and plan his educational career accordingly. A complete reappraisal of the entire educational routine presently established must be undertaken to allow a more individualized approach to each child's problem.

One innovation suggested by Katrina de Hirsch in her book *Predicting Reading Failure* is to develop transitional classes for those found to be potential classroom casualties, keeping these children off the educational merry-go-round until their level of development has progressed sufficiently through remedial correction to allow them to compete in the regular classroom. This would make obsolete the current practice of dumping every child into school, ready or not, on his sixth birthday and would take into account the fact that other factors besides calendar age are important in deciding when to start formal academic training. By evaluating each child with a relatively simple battery of de Hirsch's ten tests, the educators would be in a much better position to advise parents, and delay or alter the planned routine for each child according to his individual requirements. If this were standard school procedure, no child would need to feel embarrassed by his lack of conformity, and the stigma attached to being "different" would be lessened.

Another educational technique which has been adopted by a number of school systems in an attempt to further individualize education is the ungraded system. In this program each child is tested to determine his or her level of accomplishment and then placed in a unit with other children of equal attainment, regardless of calendar age or length of time in school. This removes a great deal of the pressure from the child since he no longer can fail a grade if he is unable to do math, reading or any other subject. He merely stays at his assigned level until he is ready to advance. He is not said to be in the third grade but is a "third-year student," and may be at a fifth-year level in math and second-year level in reading at the same time. I was quite pleased when our local schools were able to break away from tradition and adopt this new program, although it is far from ideal. Its chief deficiency comes from the fact that it is not really totally ungraded — that is, teachers still give tests, and grades, and report cards. Even though the learning-disabled child may not be in direct classroom competition at his level, he knows when he is stuck at one level and is unable to advance. Parents have complained to me that some of the teachers who have become fixed in their teaching habits seem unable to adjust to the changes, and also report that their children become more confused by having many different teachers instead of just one with whom they could become comfortably familiar. Some educators are finding that, with all its drawbacks, the old regular competitive class seems to be a better stimulus to educational advancement for some children instead of the level system which may not offer the challenge to advance.

The attempts to further individualize education and break away from the stereotyped classroom, in which the teacher stands at the front dispensing information while the children remain fixed at their desks following her every move, now appear heading in the direction of the open classroom, developed in some of the English school systems and currently being expanded in this country. In this arrangement the child becomes a much more active participant in every phase of his education, and as a participant becomes more of an active learner. Unlike the old totally permissive progressive education of some years back which became such a debacle, the open classroom is really a structured-unstructured system under direct supervision of the teacher at all times, even though the children do have a great deal to say about what they would like to study and learn. A recent CBS special television program on education dealt with an experimental open classroom program in North Dakota, and in his book *Schools Without Failure* the psychiatrist William Glasser explores the various possibilities at great length. Since the work of the Swiss psychologist Jean Piaget has developed the concept of the role of the child as an active participant in his own psychological and educational progress, it would appear that the open classroom may indeed be the wave of the future for educational systems. It will require exceptionally capable teachers with a great deal of imaginative skill, but I feel certain the challenge will be accepted and met by many of our bright young people who are now teachers or in teacher training.

But I am not an educator and certainly have no business venturing as much as a calculated guess about all these suggested innovations, even as they might affect our problem of mutual concern, the learning-disabled child. Let me go on to more familiar ground and venture an observation or two concerning the directions of future medical investigation of the child with learning disabilities and minimal brain dysfunction, for these prospects are equally exciting and challenging. Since all signs point to a biochemical basis for these disorders, the future should bring us a specific diagnostic test. This test could be used not only to confirm medical opinion but also to enable a doctor to determine which medication would be of greatest value for each individual child and how much will be needed — just as study of the blood sugar helps us treat the diabetic child. Such a diagnostic test could then be expanded to apply to early detection of minimal brain dysfunction, with the further possibility of beginning medication earlier in order to correct whatever biochemical imbalance exists even before the child is confronted with formal academic education. It would also guide us in following each child's medical progress, since we could determine the blood levels for the prescribed medication and balance them against the abnormal biochemical state. Similar studies are now being made available to help treat the epileptic child through evaluation in the blood level of the amount of anti-convulsant medication being used. As increased knowledge is obtained we could expect further studies into the genetic factors relating to minimal brain dysfunction, with enzyme determinations to detect carrier status similar to those now used in muscular dystrophy. Even intrauterine puncture before birth might be used to obtain amniotic fluid to be studied for MBD just the way it is now being used to predict possible difficulties in Rh incompatibility and other disorders. And with further investigation of the relationship of biochemical functions to all behavior perhaps a more intensive study of minimal brain dysfunction will open the door to better understanding of many conditions that are now labeled as emotional or mental diseases.

There are other difficulties that appear to be related to minimal brain dysfunction which the physician needs to study more intently. What is the relationship of allergy to MBD? Why do so many of these children come in with a history of repeated formula changes as infants or continuing difficulty requiring lengthy courses of injections for allergy? Is it really an allergy or a disorder of the autonomic nervous system? What about the increased incidence of bed-wetting, colic, even ulcers? Is there some common denominator that has escaped us? What is the relationship of MBD with other neurological disorders, such as epilepsy or the various speech disorders we now group under the term aphasias? Will the new experimental studies with the EEG, using what is called evoked potentials, prove of practical clinical value? And what factors determine the course that one particular child will take, be it hyperactivity or hypoactivity? All of these stand out as future challenges for scientific investigation.

Equally as important as the obligations of educators and physicians to the LD child are the responsibilities of workers in the behavioral sciences. They must also cast aside the superstitions and prejudices that have hampered advancement in the study of MBD and assume their rightful role as valuable consultants to the learning disability team. The future may or may not bring all the advances just mentioned, but the present is here with us now. In a recent article in *The New York Times* on the link between learning disorders and delinquency, it was stated that as many as eighty percent of delinquents may disclose a history of difficulty in learning to read, and this fact can no longer be dismissed as coincidental. It must alert us to the necessity of assuming a close relationship and cause us to act accordingly. The problems of juvenile delinquency are complex and difficult, and every youngster with a behavioral disorder may not have MBD (nor does every child with MBD become a delinquent). But on the basis of the knowledge now at hand, it would seem much more logical to study the offender from the standpoint of possible MBD rather than always to assume that his environment was the only cause of delinquency. Millions of dollars have been spent on the assumption that juvenile delinquency was exclusively a socio-cultural disorder correctable by altering or removing the environmental deficiencies, but the problem looms as large as ever. We need to begin at the very onset — in the early years of schooling, with better teaching certainly, and with better future occupational prospects for all children of all classes. These opportunities, however, will always be denied to the child who cannot read or learn, and he knows it only too well. The psychologist needs to impart an awareness of this aspect of the problem to all who deal with the juvenile offender — the school counselor or principal (or the assistant principal, since the role of disciplinarian usually falls to him), the judge or probation officer from the juvenile court, the vocational rehabilitation officer, the child's minister (who can be a tremendous source of help to both the child and his parents), and all the others who deal with him when he runs afoul of the law. An excellent work dealing with all the various aspects of these problems is *Helping the Adolescent with the Hidden Handicap* edited by Lauriel E. Anderson.

An interesting point that has emerged in discussing family histories with the parents of learning-disabled children has been the prevalence of emotional disorders in the adults of the family. If we are to learn more about the relationship of these disorders, those who deal with adults will need to stress this part of the individual's development much more than has been done in the past under the influence of the "dynamic" theories of psychiatry which have overstressed the importance of early parental mistreatment almost to the exclusion of any other possible causative factors. I recently discussed this with one of my psychiatric colleagues who said, "When I first became interested in psychiatry I believed that most mental disorders were organic, then I wandered off and listened to all this environmental theory, but I'm coming back now to where I started." Fortunately, this attitude is being adopted by more and more physicians who have become disenchanted with the inappropriateness of the whole concept of infantile sexual maladjustment as the explanation for childhood behavioral disorders. As they begin to influence their co-workers in the guidance clinics and mental health centers we will see a much sounder approach to the problem of the child with learning disability.

Another problem that must be dealt with now is the LD adolescent or young adult who recognizes the importance of advanced education and who is anxious to go on, but finds that few colleges or universities are able to help him. Just as in the elementary grades, the entrance requirements are fixed and the curriculum is firmly established. The learning-disabled adolescent who has managed to struggle through it all and graduate from high school finds a new series of disappointments are in store for him. If he doesn't score well on his SAT or ACT or whatever other irrevocable authority the college of his choice uses to limit its enrollments, he will find that his grades will be unacceptable to all but a few of the institutions of higher learning. If he does manage to make the freshman class in one of these, he will most often find exactly what he has found before — the classroom routine is predetermined for the eighty percent who have no learning disability, and little account is taken of individual variations. If he felt lost in the shuffle before because he couldn't figure out what was going on, he really finds it worse now, for the crush in our larger institutions is overwhelming enough for any student, much less a learning-disabled one. The young adult with MBD once again faces failure and humiliation, and once again he has no place to turn to.

While there is no disgrace attached to not having a college degree, the stress on the importance of this achievement is pounded into our youth from an early age. To be told he is not college material, or to have another experience of failure is not likely to enhance the low self-esteem and feeling of inferiority which the LD youngster already possesses. If his ambitions exceed pumping gasoline at a filling station or driving a delivery truck, he finds two avenues open to him — a business college, which usually has just enough math to restrain him, or a trade school, actually developed for the retarded, which will train him for an occupation provided he can use his hands skillfully. This shuts the door on many an MBD youngster, since manual dexterity is not his strong point.

Fortunately a number of institutions of higher learning are beginning to recognize the individual capabilities of young people who are learning-disabled, and are willing to accept the responsibility of giving them an opportunity to learn by doing without penalizing them for their difficulties in obtaining abstract knowledge from a book. One such school with which I am personally familiar is a technical institute located in one of the states neighboring mine. Here practical education in career preparation is stressed and a sufficiently diverse choice is offered to appeal to individual preferences, such as cosmetology, practical nursing, food and restaurant management, police science, medical technology, and dental hygiene, as well as the usual mechanical courses. In discussing their educational philosophy with the various faculty members that I met, I found that they were concerned with the vital importance of skilled technicians in the world today and had an increasing awareness of the educational imbalance which yearly produces thousands of young adults with degrees in the humanities or liberal arts who are unable to get a job or find any practical use for their advanced knowledge. Again, not every student at the technical institutions has a learning disability, nor is every individual able to succeed in a technical course, for the courses are not simple and do require conscientious application and devotion of purpose. They do, however, stress practical application of the materials being taught rather than penalize the student for his inability to express his knowledge in writing through a formal examination. I am certain that there are many other institutions similar to this school throughout the country, and it is most gratifying to find that the attitude in higher educational circles is beginning to swing in this direction. All is not hopeless for our current crop of learning-disabled adolescents and young adults who lost the chance for early recognition and treatment of their disability in the first few grades.

So here stands Steve — at the real crossroads of his young life. The future for him may hold disappointment and failure, or achievement and success. There are many doors which will remain closed to him, but he will find new ones opening up along the way. Those who are to help him — teachers, parents, physicians, and their allies — can expect to encounter many difficulties, but for them, too, the future seems brighter. Years ago Victor Hugo wrote that nothing in the world was more powerful than "an idea whose time has come." Let us hope that for Steve, and his eight million first cousins, the understanding of the concept of specific learning disability due to minimal brain dysfunction has come at last, and that with acceptance and understanding of the true nature of the disorder, the learning disability team can join forces to help each "square peg" achieve his rightful place as a contributing member of society.

SUGGESTED ADDITIONAL READING

The surge of interest in learning disabilities has produced so many new books and other writings that it is almost impossible for anyone to keep up with them all. The works mentioned here are the ones that I personally have found most helpful in trying to understand learning-disabled children, and the ones that I have found most useful to recommend to parents and teachers who wish to learn more about their particular interest. Omission of any one book should not be considered a rejection of its value but in all probability simply represents an oversight on my part.

Associations

Teachers and parents who wish to have access to a more current and complete bibliography should write to the following organizations, or write to your own related state or local chapter. And if you can't find one, why not get things going and start one yourself?

The Association for Children with Learning Disabilities
2200 Brownsville Road
Pittsburgh, Pennsylvania 15210

California Association for Neurologically
    Handicapped Children
11291 McNab Street
Garden Grove, California 92641

Canadian Association for Children with
    Learning Disabilities
687 Briar Hill Road
Toronto 19, Canada

New Jersey Association for Brain Injured Children
61 Lincoln Street
East Orange, New Jersey 07017

New York Association for Brain Injured Children
305 Broadway
New York, New York 10007

National Easter Seal Society for Crippled
    Children and Adults
2023 West Ogden Avenue
Chicago, Illinois 60612

United Cerebral Palsy Association
66 East 34th Street
New York, New York 10016

Other organizations concerned with learning disability include the following.

The Council for Exceptional Children
1411 South Jefferson Davis Highway
Arlington, Virginia 22202
Publication: *Exceptional Children*
(Teachers can join the Division of Learning Disabilities of the CEC.)

Association for Childhood Education International
3615 Wisconsin Avenue, N.W.
Washington, D.C. 20016
Publication: *Childhood Education*

The Orton Society
8415 Bellona Lane
Towson, Maryland 21204
Publication: *Bulletin of the Orton Society*

Current interest at the national level is evidenced by the establishment of the National Special Education Information Center, which can be reached by writing to "Closer Look," Box 1492, Washington, D.C. 20013.

Journals

In addition to the publications noted above readers may wish to subscribe to two excellent journals which cover the entire field of learning disabilities.

> *Academic Therapy*, a Quarterly
> Academic Therapy Publications
> 1539 Fourth Street
> San Rafael, California 94901
> (also publishes a newsletter, "Interim")

> *The Journal of Learning Disabilities*
> The Professional Press
> 5 North Wabash Avenue
> Chicago, Illinois 60602

The Task Force Monographs

TASK FORCE ONE: Clements, Sam D., ed., "Minimal Brain Dysfunction in Children: Terminology and Identification," NINDB Monograph #3, PHS Bulletin #1415, Washington, US Dept of HEW, 1966. $0.20.

TASK FORCE TWO: Haring, Norris G., ed., Minimal Brain Dysfunction in Children: Educational, Medical and Health Related Services," N & S DCP Monograph, PHS Publication #2015, US Dept of HEW, 1969. $1.00.

TASK FORCE THREE: Chalfant, Jas. C. and Scheffelin, Margaret A., eds., "Central Processing Dysfunctions in Children: A Review of Research," NINDS Monograph #9, US Dept of HEW, 1969. $1.25.

All three of the monographs may be obtained from the Superintendent of Documents, US Government Printing Office, Washington, D. C. 20402. Number One represents the best twenty-cent investment any parent or teacher can make, for it gives an excellent introduction to the entire problem. Number Two will interest educators and physicians, and Number Three, while rather heavy reading, will give the reader an intensive coverage of experimental theory.

THE CLASSICS

These are the works which form the foundation for our current understanding of minimal brain dysfunction and specific learning disability, and, while much of their material now is of historical interest only, they afford the beginning student a basis for further study and investigation.

Psychopathology and Education of the Brain-Injured Child, Vol. I, *Fundamentals and Treatment*, by Alfred A. Strauss and Laura E. Lehtinen. New York, Grune and Stratton, 1947. Vol. II, *Progress in Theory and Clinic*, by Alfred A. Strauss and Newell C. Kephart. New York, Grune and Stratton, 1955.

These are the basic works which introduced the concepts of perceptual disturbances and behavior alterations considered characteristic of MBD, and laid the groundwork for the progress that has followed. Dr. Strauss himself told me he regretted using the term "brain-injured," but his pioneering studies will be remembered long after the disputes over semantics and etiology have subsided. Perhaps the suggestion that we call this disorder the "Strauss Syndrome" after this giant of child neurology is not an unseemly recommendation after all.

The Other Child: The Brain-Injured Child, by Richard S. Lewis, with Alfred A. Strauss and Laura E. Lehtinen. New York, Grune and Stratton, 1st ed., 1951, 2nd (enlarged) ed., 1960.

The first authoritative work for parents to help them understand why their LD children behave the way they do. After twenty years, this is still an excellent source of information for all interested, whether we call him an "other child" or a "square peg."

Cerebral Palsy and Related Disorders: A Developmental Approach to Dysfunction, by Eric Denhoff and Isabel P. Robinault. New York, McGraw-Hill, 1960.

The first comprehensive study to propose the concept of "dysfunction" to encompass all the disorders of the child's developing central nervous system which show the characteristics we now attribute to MBD; this fine work also gives some excellent recommendations for handling and treatment of the LD child.

Brain Damage in Children: The biological and social aspects, edited by Herbert G. Birch. Baltimore, Williams and Wilkins, 1964.

The proceedings of a conference held at Children's Hospital in Philadelphia in November of 1962, ably edited by Dr. Birch who has long been regarded as an outstanding authority in this field. His own introductory chapter, as well as the one by Leon Eisenberg about behavioral manifestations and the one by Howard Kelman about the effect of the child on the family, make excellent reading.

Reading, Writing and Speech Disorders in Children, by Samuel T. Orton. New York, W. W. Norton, 1937, 2nd ed. 1961.

This is the pioneering work by the real "father". of learning disabilities, and, although some of his concepts have been discarded in the light of more recent research and understandings, his observations of the children under his care are just as valid as they were thirty-five years ago. Every true student of dyslexia and other learning difficulties should include Orton on his reference shelf.

Developmental Diagnosis: Normal and Abnormal Child Development, by Arnold Gesell and Catherine S. Armatruda. New York, Paul B. Hoeber, 2nd ed. 1947.

While not specifically concerned with MBD or learning disability, this work by the first real authority on child development must be included as a point of departure in the study of variations and abnormalities in developmental maturation.

Auditory Disorders in Children: A Manual for Differential Diagnosis, by Helmer Myklebust. New York, Grune and Stratton, 1954.

Another work not specifically concerned with learning disability as such, this early study by another great in the learning disability field gives the author's observations concerning the similarities and differences shown in behavior by children with communication problems due to deficient hearing (peripheral deafness), mental deficiency, emotional (psychic) deafness and aphasia (minimal brain dysfunction). This is the first in a long series of valuable contributions made by Dr. Myklebust.

OF GENERAL INTEREST

Children with Learning Disabilities: Theories, Diagnosis, and Teaching Strategies, by Janet W. Lerner. Boston, Houghton Mifflin, 1971.

It is difficult to select any one book as the best of the lot, but if I had to make such a choice, this would be it. Dr. Lerner has written a well-organized book covering every aspect of the learning disability field, including a most acceptable presentation of the medical considerations. She discusses diagnostic testing and methods of clinical teaching involved in each of the theoretical approaches to learning disabilities: sensory-motor, perceptual-motor, perceptual, linguistic, and cognitive. There is an excellent chapter on the maturational, psychological and social factors concerned, and the final section on facilities and programs for teaching children with learning disabilities should be a must for all educators responsible for such activities. The bibliography is unusually complete and the listing of materials available and their sources in the appendix is thorough and comprehensive.

Progress in Learning Disabilities, edited by Helmer R. Myklebust. New York, Grune and Stratton, Vol. 1, 1968; Vol. 2, 1971.

Two outstanding compilations of papers covering every aspect of learning disabilities in depth. In Volume 1 I found the chapters by Norman Geschwind on neurological foundations of language and Beale Ong on the pediatrician's role in learning disabilities most helpful, while Marianna Frostig's chapter on education, including her testing routine, should be of inestimable value to teachers. The work of R. A. Dykman and his associates designating the primary defect in learning disabilities as an "attentional deficit syndrome" highlights Volume 2, which also contains Elena Boder's discussion of her diagnostic approach to the three forms of dyslexia and an excellent chapter on early childhood education by Eric Denhoff and the Hainsworths. Both of these volumes belong in every school library, especially the colleges concerned with educating our teachers.

Learning Disabilities: Introduction to Educational and Medical Management, edited by Lester Tarnopol. Springfield, C. C. Thomas, 1971.

Learning Disorders in Children: Diagnosis, Medication and Education, edited by Lester Tarnopol. Boston, Little, Brown, 1971.

These are two more excellent works, both compilations of papers presented at symposia sponsored by the San Francisco chapter of the California Association for Neurologically Handicapped Children, ably edited by Dr. Tarnopol who is uniquely listed as an "engineering psychologist." In the first work I found the chapters by Helen Gofman on the physician's role and Leslie Knott on rehabilitation and the community most helpful. Barbara Bateman presents an interesting section on a controversial view of reading, and Dr. Tarnopol himself makes an outstanding contribution on delinquency and learning disability. The second volume gives an almost verbatim transcript of an enlightening discussion of medical treatment by all the authorities involved, and the chapter on neurology by Calanchini and Trout alone is worth the price of the book.

ALL ABOUT DYSLEXIA AND READING PROBLEMS

The Disabled Reader: Education of the Dyslexic Child, edited by John Money. Baltimore, Johns Hopkins Press, 1966.

The best and most comprehensive of all the works about reading disorders per se, presenting in the first section several excellent works of theoretical interest, while the last section gives detailed accounts of specific remedial techniques, including an excellent critique on the teaching of reading by Thomas J. Edwards. There is a comprehensive appendix of working materials and a complete bibliography of tests used. Dr. Money has also edited an earlier work, *Reading Disability: Progress and Research Needs in Dyslexia.* Baltimore, Johns Hopkins Press, 1962.

The Dyslexic Child, by Macdonald Critchley. Springfield, C. C. Thomas, 1970.
A small but excellent volume by an outstanding British authority, updating his previous work published in 1964 under the title of *Developmental Dyslexia.*

Dyslexia: Diagnosis and Treatment of Reading Disorders, edited by Arthur H. and Virginia T. Keeney. St. Louis, C. V. Mosby, 1968.
The entire proceedings of the National Conference on Dyslexia held in Philadelphia in 1966 which I had the privilege of attending; this volume contains contributions by Critchley, de Hirsch, Bender, Cruickshank, and Goldberg as well as a number of other authorities. Dr. Critchley's "seventeen topics worthy of research" are most thought-provoking.

Reading Disability: Developmental Dyslexia, by Lloyd C. Thompson. Springfield, C. C. Thomas, 1969.
A very well-written work clearly presented, concentrating on reading difficulties. The historical aspects of our understanding of dyslexia are well covered, and there is a useful bibliography for further reference.

Current Concepts in Dyslexia, edited by Jack Hartsein. St. Louis, C. V. Mosby, 1971.
One of the better new works, edited by an ophthalmologist, and containing an excellent chapter on the role of the reading teacher by R. W. Burnett, and a sound presentation on education of learning-disabled children by Eleanore T. Kenney. I was disap-

pointed in the last two chapters on the medical aspects, although the discussion of behavior modification by H. E. Cantor is well presented.

ESPECIALLY FOR THE TEACHERS

Predicting Reading Failure, by Katrina de Hirsch, Jeannette Jansky, and William S. Langford. New York, Harper and Row, 1966.

An in-depth study of a group of children evaluated at the kindergarten level and followed through the second-grade level, using a battery of over thirty different tests and demonstrating the use of ten with a high degree of accuracy in assessing future academic difficulties. Each test is explained completely and the author's methods clearly presented. I would recommend this work highly to every kindergarten and primary grade teacher.

Learning Disabilities: Educational Principles and Practices, Doris J. Johnson and Helmer R. Myklebust. New York, Grune and Stratton, 1967.

Another valuable work reflecting Dr. Myklebust's theories and Dr. Johnson's practical educational advice, with a complete presentation of remedial techniques for all aspects of learning disabilities.

Educating Children with Learning Disabilities, edited by Edward C. Frierson and Walter B. Barbe. New York, Appleton-Crofts, 1967.

An outstanding selection of scientific papers on all aspects of learning disabilities, including works by Strauss, Clements, Myklebust, Eisenberg and a number of others.

Children with Learning Disabilities: A Five Year Follow-up Study, by Elizabeth M. Koppitz. New York, Grune and Stratton, 1971.

A realistic and sober appraisal of the status of special classes and programs for learning-disabled children, presenting the results of the author's observations on 177 pupils enrolled in a public-school learning-disability program. Early identification and individual flexibility are stressed and the total effectiveness of all the procedures is carefully scrutinized. This book should be read by educators charged with the responsibility of developing new LD programs, especially those who are convinced that one or two years of special education will cure the learning-disabled child of his problems.

Schools Without Failure, by William Glasser. New York, Harper and Row, 1969.

A stimulating work presenting a strong case for abandoning our stereotyped classroom teaching in favor of more active participation in learning experiences by the children themselves. This book is written by a psychiatrist whose previous study, *Reality Therapy,* did so much to debunk psychoanalytic theory and place the treatment of emotional problems on a more practical basis.

Understanding Piaget: An Introduction to Children's Cognitive Development, by Mary Ann Spencer Pulaski. New York, Harper and Row, 1971.

This could almost be considered a companion work to the preceding book, for it presents the theories and observations of the Swiss psychologist Jean Piaget who has stressed the importance of the active role of the child in his own maturation. The discussion of the role of language and communication is especially pertinent to learning disabilities.

MORE ON REMEDIAL TEACHING

A *Teaching Method for Brain-Injured and Hyperactive Children,* by William M. Cruickshank. Syracuse, Syracuse University Press, 1961.

The Teacher of Brain-Injured Children, edited by William M. Cruickshank. Syracuse, Syracuse University Press, 1966.

A leading authority on education of learning-disabled children shares his remarkable insight and valuable experience.

Learning Disabilities, by James J. McCarthy and Joan F. Mc-
Carthy. Boston, Allyn and Bacon, 1969.

A compact but thorough presentation of thirteen different
methods for handling the educational problems of the learning-
disabled child.

Remedial Techniques in Basic School Subjects, by Grace Fernald.
New York, McGraw-Hill, 1943.

This might well have been included among the classics in the
field, since it is a pioneering work on the use of the multi-sensory
approach in helping the child with learning disability.

A *Programmed Primer in Learning Disabilities,* by Jerome A.
Kroth. Springfield, C. C. Thomas, 1971.

A complete presentation giving the essentials in diagnosis and
remediation techniques using the teaching machine.

Teaching Inefficient Learners, by Wineva M. Grzynkowicz.
Springfield, C. C. Thomas, 1971.

Another thorough manual of remediation techniques, but what
I enjoyed most were the author's own pungent comments: "A
child does not come to school labelled and classified, and it often
takes educators two or three years to condition him so that he
will fit into one of our preestablished categories," and "Most
children enter school expecting to learn until we use the first
six weeks to destroy this idea. . . . Rather than adjust our curriculum and our educational objectives to him and his needs we
start him on his path to underachiever which will be perpetrated
throughout his school life." Anyone who writes like that is on
our side!

Principles of Childhood Disabilities, edited by John V. Irwin and
Michael Marge. New York, Appleton-Century-Crofts, 1972.

This book was published almost too late to be reviewed, but I
must mention the chapter on Social Management (pp. 355–391)
by Empress Y. Zedler. I am certain that parents and teachers will
find Dr. Zedler's discussion of affection (interpersonal satisfaction), acceptance (group status), and approval (personal worth
and self-development) of tremendous value in the day-by-day

practical handling of the difficulties confronting the learning-disabled child in the educational establishment.

TESTING

Wechsler Intelligence Scale for Children, by David Wechsler. New York, The Psychological Corp., 1955.

Stanford-Binet Intelligence Scales, by L. M. Terman and M. A. Merrill. Boston, Houghton-Mifflin, 1960.

The Illinois Test of Psycholinguistic Abilities, by S. A. Kirk, J. P. McCarthy and W. D. Kirsch. Rev. ed. Urbana, Illinois, University of Illinois Press, 1968.

A Visual Motor Gestalt Test and Its Clinical Use, by Lauretta Bender. New York, The American Orthopsychiatric Assn. Research Monograph No. 3, 1938.

The Bender Gestalt Test for Young Children, by Elizabeth M. Koppitz. New York, Grune and Stratton, 1964.

Wepman Test of Auditory Discrimination, by J. Wepman. Chicago, Language Research Associates, 1958.

The Marianne Frostig Developmental Test of Visual Perception, by M. Frostig, P. Maslow, D. Lefever, and J. Whittlesey. Palo Alto, Consulting Psychologists Press, 1964.

Draw a Person Test: The Measurement of Intelligence by Drawings, by Frances Goodenough. Yonkers-on-Hudson, World, 1962.

Wide Range Achievement Test, by J. F. Jastak, S. W. Bijou, and S. R. Jastak. Wilmington, Guidance Associates, 1965.

ESPECIALLY FOR PARENTS

The Brain-Injured Child in Home, School and Community, by William M. Cruickshank. Syracuse, Syracuse University Press, 1967.

A warm and understanding yet realistic and competent study by one of the educational giants in the field of learning disability.

Learning Disabilities: Its Implications to a Responsible Society,
   compiled and edited by Doreen Kronick. Chicago, Developmental Learning Materials, 1969.

A fine little volume presenting the views of seven authorities on
different aspects of the LD problem. I found Sol Gordon's chapter on the psychological problems of adolescents most valuable
and Mrs. Kronick (a Founder of the Canadian ACLD) has contributed three chapters including the provocative "What Is Success?"

Helping the Adolescent with the Hidden Handicap, edited by
   Lauriel E. Anderson. Published by Academic Therapy Publications, 1970, and available through the Los Angeles Office
   of CANHC, P. O. Box 604, Los Angeles, Calif. 90053.

Another small volume filled with practical advice for parents
and all those interested in the LD child whose identification may
have come too late. Read "The NH Adolescent and Juvenile
Law" by William Mulligan and "Reversing a Negative Self-
Image" by Sol Gordon for some interesting insights.

*The Waysiders: A New Approach to Reading and the Dyslexic
   Child*, by R. M. N. Crosby with R. A. Liston. New York,
   Delacorte Press, 1968.

An interesting presentation of the author's views on reading
disability and his suggestions to parents for helping their children.

A Parent's Guide to Learning Problems, by Margaret Golick.
   Available through the Quebec ACLD, P. O. Box 22, Cote St.
   Luc Postal Station, Montreal, Quebec, Canada.

This excellent report, which was reprinted in the June, 1968,
issue of the *Journal of Learning Disabilities* (1: 24:35, 1968),
should be in the hands of every parent of a learning-disabled
child.

Teacher and Child: A Book for Parents and Teachers, by Haim
   G. Ginott. New York, Macmillan, 1972.

Although he doesn't actually mention learning disability and
MBD, any parent can recognize the children Dr. Ginott is dis-

cussing when he reports on the humiliating sarcasm all too frequently meted out in the classroom and at home to these unfortunates. It may be difficult to always maintain the calm attitude proposed by this popular psychologist, but his respect for the dignity and self-esteem so important to the developing child is worthy of consideration. Buy this book — read it yourself — then lend or give it to your child's teacher. One doesn't have to have a special degree to be humane and understanding — and what dividends it brings to the learning-disabled child!

Cradles of Eminence, by Victor and Mildred Goertzel. Boston, Little, Brown, 1962.
Not really a book about learning disability, but the accounts of the early educational problems of Wilson, Edison, Einstein, Zola and others are bound to bring a sympathetic and perhaps encouraging response from the parents of LD children.

ESPECIALLY FOR PHYSICIANS

Minimal Brain Dysfunction in Children, by Paul H. Wender. New York, Wiley, 1971.
This is the book that makes me feel "I wish I had said that," for Dr. Wender's excellent presentation covers the medical and biochemical aspects of MBD and SLD better than any other I have found. The author categorically states that MBD is the most frequent cause of referral to child guidance clinics, and rebukes those who would withhold medical treatment in favor of the ineffectual conventional methods of psychotherapy. The suggestions as to the cause and proper handling of the problems of the child with MBD are clearly documented.

Minimal Cerebral Dysfunction, edited by Martin Bax and Ronald MacKeith. London, Wm. Heinemann, 1963.
A compilation of the papers presented at an international study group in Oxford which proposed the discarding of the term "brain damage" and covered the many aspects of MBD.

Neurological Examination of Children, by Richmond S. Paine and Thomas E. Oppe. London, Wm. Heinemann, 1966.

A practical text covering all aspects of pediatric neurology; Chapter VII ("Special Tests of Cerebral Function") is especially applicable to the child with MBD.

Behavioral Science in Pediatric Medicine, edited by N. B. Talbot, J. Kagen, and L. Eisenberg. Philadelphia, W. B. Saunders, 1971.

An excellent new work with outstanding chapters on physiological psychology covering learning and intellectual behavior (by A. F. Mirsky), perception (by R. H. Forgus), learning (by S. H. White) and psychopharmacology in childhood (by Eisenberg).

Man and Memory, by D. S. Halacy, Jr. New York, Harper and Row, 1970.

A fascinating book which reads like a detective novel, discussing the mysteries of the as yet undiscovered functions of the human mind; important to the understanding of learning disability since memory is so intensely involved in the acquisition and retention of knowledge.

Drugs, Development, and Cerebral Function, edited by W. Lynn Smith. Springfield, C. C. Thomas, 1970.

Catecholamines, by R. J. Wurtman. Boston, Little, Brown, 1966.

Two volumes that can help the physician understand the biochemical aspects of learning and behavior, and their relationship to MBD.

In addition to the above books there are a number of other publications available to physicians who are interested in learning more about MBD and the children who make up this important segment of pediatric practice. The entire August, 1968, issue of *Pediatric Clinics of North America* was devoted to a symposium on developmental disturbances of motility and language, including a chapter on the syndrome of minimal cerebral damage by Richmond S. Paine. Two entire issues of a new publication,

Current Problems in Pediatrics were devoted to learning and language disorders in the pre-school child (August, 1971) and the school-age child (September, 1971); edited by Helen F. Gofman and B. W. Allmond, Jr. these two studies cover the entire field of the application of medicine to learning disabilities. Recently Ross Laboratories distributed to physicians the report of the Sixty-first Ross Conference on Pediatric Research entitled "Learning Disorders in Children," edited by J. H. Menkes and R. J. Schain and giving a comprehensive picture of the entire MBD problem and its medical treatment. The Ciba Pharmaceutical Company has produced a monograph entitled "The Hyperactive Child" which covers this topic exceptionally well. The entire November, 1971, issue of the *Journal of Learning Disabilities* was devoted to the use of medication in the treatment of the LD child, and the May, 1972, issue of *Pediatrics* contained a report of the symposium on behavior modification through the use of medication held by the American Academy of Pediatrics (see Eisenberg 49: 709–715, 1972).

I should like to mention some other articles which will be useful to the physician in helping him to understand and treat the child with MBD:

Nichamin, S. J. and Barahal, G. D., "Faulty Neurological Integration with Perceptual Disorders in Children — An Abridged Treatment Approach; A Two-Dimensional Program of Methylphenidate and Psychologic Management," *Michigan Medicine* 67: 1071–1075, 1968.

Dr. Nichamin's grasp of the problems encountered by the physician in helping the child with MBD and his practical combination of medication and counselling closely parallels my own experience. This report which indicated that his overall results were so successful did much to encourage me to continue my own efforts.

Clements, S. D. and Peters, J. E., "Minimal Brain Dysfunction in the School Age Child," *Archives of General Psychiatry* 6: 185–197, 1962.

This removed the problem of the MBD child from the realm

of parental mishandling and placed it on an organic basis where it belongs.

Millichap, J. G., "Drugs in the Management of Hyperactive and Perceptually Handicapped Children," *Journal of the American Medical Association* 206: 1527–1530, 1968.
This comprehensive study was an introduction to methylphenidate and its value as a first consideration in the treatment of MBD.

Huessy, H. R. and Wright, Alice, "The Use of Imipramine in Children's Behavior Disorders," *Acta Paedopsychiatra* (Basel) 37: 194–199, 1970.
This work introduced me to the use of another valuable medication that I have found most effective in the treatment of MBD.

Silver, L. B., "A Proposed View on the Etiology of the Neurological Learning Disability Syndrome," *Journal of Learning Disabilities* 4: 123–133, 1971.
Snyder, S. H., "New Developments in Brain Chemistry: Catecholamine Metabolism and the Action of Psychotropic Drugs," *American Journal of Orthopsychiatry* 37: 864–879, 1967.
These two articles are almost companion pieces, explaining the currently accepted theories concerning the cause of MBD and associated learning disabilities as a biochemical disturbance, and the corrective action of the medications being used.

"Report of the Conference on the Use of Stimulant Drugs in the Treatment of Behaviorally Disturbed Young School Children" (Jan. 11–12, 1971). Washington, D. C., Office of Child Development, US Dept of HEW.
"Federal Involvement in the Use of Behavior Modification Drugs on Grammar School Children of the Right to Privacy Inquiry." Hearing before a Subcommittee of the Committee on Government Operations, House of Representatives, on Sept. 29, 1970. Supt. of Documents, US Government Printing Office, Washington, D. C. 20402.

Two additional recent publications by governmental agencies concerned with learning-disabled children and their management.

"Evoked Potentials and Human Intelligence," *Final Report,* Project No. 6–1545. Washington: October, 1968, US Dept of HEW, Office of Education, Bureau of Research.

A study on experiments to detect MBD, using the electro-encephalograph.

Facts on Quacks — What You Should Know About Health Quackery. Published by the American Medical Association, Department of Health Education, 535 N. Dearborn Street, Chicago, Illinois 60610.

This pamphlet should be of value not only to parents of learning-disabled children but also to patients who may be taken advantage of by false claimants for treatment of arthritis, cancer, overweight, and other medical problems.

INDEX